The Catholic Imagination

The
Catholic
Imagination

Andrew Greeley

UNIVERSITY OF CALIFORNIA PRESS

Berkeley   Los Angeles   London

The frontispiece is a detail from *Virgin and the Child*,
attributed to Raphael. Courtesy CORBIS/Bettmann.

University of California Press
Berkeley and Los Angeles, California

University of California Press, Ltd.
London, England

First paperback printing 2001

© 2000 by the Regents of the University of California

Library of Congress Cataloging-in-Publication Data

Greeley, Andrew M., 1928–
    The Catholic imagination / Andrew Greeley.
        p.   cm.
    Includes bibliographical references and index.
    ISBN 978-0-520-23204-4 (pbk. : alk. paper)
        1. Catholic Church—Doctrines.   2. Theology, Doctrinal
Popular works.   I. Title.
BX1754.G697   2000
282—dc21   99-33945
                                                            CIP

Printed in the United States of America

16   15   14   13   12   11
10   9   8   7   6

The paper used in this publication meets the minimum
requirements of ANSI/NISO Z39.48-1992 (R 1997)
(*Permanence of Paper*). ∞

For David Tracy,
theologian of the Enchanted Imagination

Religions commit suicide when they find
their inspiration in dogma.

Alfred North Whitehead

Imagination is a representation of what
Eternally exists, really and unchangeably.

William Blake

CONTENTS

INTRODUCTION
The Sacraments of Sensibility
1

CHAPTER ONE
Sacred Place, Sacred Time
23

CHAPTER TWO
Sacred Desire
55

CHAPTER THREE
The Mother Love of God
89

CHAPTER FOUR
Community
111

CHAPTER FIVE

Hierarchy

137

CHAPTER SIX

Salvation

159

CHAPTER SEVEN

Sensibility and Socialization

173

CONCLUSION

The Enchanted Imagination

183

A Note on Sources

189

Notes

191

Index

199

The Sacraments
of Sensibility

Catholics live in an enchanted world, a world of statues and holy water, stained glass and votive candles, saints and religious medals, rosary beads and holy pictures. But these Catholic paraphernalia are mere hints of a deeper and more pervasive religious sensibility which inclines Catholics to see the Holy lurking in creation. As Catholics, we find our houses and our world haunted by a sense that the objects, events, and persons of daily life are revelations of grace.

The assertions in the last paragraph are not statements of what Catholics should be like, nor are they demands that Catholics return to earlier modes of religious sensibility. They are, as I hope to show in this extended essay, factual descriptions of Catholics, both practicing and supposedly lapsed, and the Catholic religious imagination that shapes their lives.

This special Catholic imagination can appropriately be called sacramental. It sees created reality as a "sacrament," that is, a revelation of the presence of God. The workings of this imagination are most obvious in the Church's seven sacraments, but the seven are both a result and a reinforcement of a much broader Catholic view of reality. And Reality. Andre Dubus, who has an acute awareness of sacramentality, describes this perspective in his book *Meditations from a Moving Chair*: "A sacrament is physical and within it is God's love; as a sandwich is physical, and nutritious, and pleasurable, and within it is love, if someone makes it for you and gives it to you with love; even harried or tired or impatient love, but with love's direction and concern, love's again and again wavering and distorted focus on goodness, then God's love too is in the sandwich."

The sandwich becomes enchanted because it is permeated by, dense in, awash with the two loves—human and divine.

How can a large group of people accept an enchanted cosmos when in fact Creation has been demystified and demythologized? Does not disenchantment rule the modern world? Or could it be that the enchanted Catholic imagination is indeed a manifestation of post-modernity?

I don't believe in either modernity or post-modernity. I find no persuasive evidence that either modern or post-modern humankind exists outside of faculty office buildings. Everyone tends to be pre-modern.[1] There may well be a theoretical opposition between enchantment and science, though such scientific phenomena as black holes, dark space, the nonlocality of particles, big bang inflation, and the great attractor suggest that science may have an enchantment of its own. For the purposes of this book, I intend to concentrate on Catholic manifestations of the enchanted imagination because I find ample evidence that most humans (other than philosophers and theologians) see little inconsistency between science and religion in their ordinary lives.

Is this special Catholic sensibility gradually declining in the face of long-term trends of demystification and secularization? Certainly, in the years since the Second Vatican Council, some Catholic ideologues have tried to demystify the Catholic heritage in order to make it more palatable to moderns. They have not been successful, however, as I will try to show in the chapter on Mary, the mother of Jesus. I am not persuaded that there is any evidence that shows a decline in mystery. Indeed, it appears that belief in life after death has increased by 20 percent when U.S. Catholics born in the early decades of this century are compared to U.S. Catholics born since 1940.

I realize that these assumptions go against the existing conventional wisdom. I take issue with that supposed wisdom in my book *Religion as Poetry*. I will not pause here to address it again.

In this extended essay I will ask whether one can derive from works of high culture (ecclesiastical architecture, opera, painting) permeated by Catholic sensibility hypotheses which predict the way ordinary Catholics behave and then test these hypotheses against empirical data. Does the sensibility displayed by Catholic high art also reveal itself in the attitudes and behavior of ordinary Catholics? If Catholic high culture is enchanted, can one find the same enchantment in the lives of the Catholic laity? In a further attempt to demonstrate the power of the Catholic imagination, even for Catholics who may have officially left the Church—what we might call "cultural Catholics"—I will explore whether the sensibility expressed in Catholic high culture continues to influence Catholic popular culture and artists who are not known for their explicit piety.

I endorse Alfred North Whitehead's comment in the epigraph, but I do not wish thereby to reject dogma even if it is the superstructure of religion. Religion begins in the imagination and in stories, but it cannot remain there. The stories which are our first contact with religion ("A decree went out from Caesar that the whole world should be enrolled..." "Early on the morning the first day of the week..." "And Jesus took bread and blessed it...") are subject to rational and critical examination as we grow older to discover both what they mean and whether we are still able to believe them. Bethlehem becomes the Incarnation. The empty tomb becomes the Resurrection. The final supper becomes the Eucharist. These are all necessary and praiseworthy developments. Nonetheless, the origins and raw power of religion are at the imaginative (that is, experiential and narrative) level both for the individual and for the tradition.[2] The doctrine of the Incarnation has less appeal to the whole self than does the picture of the Madonna and Child in a cave. The doctrine of the Resurrection has less appeal to the total human personality than do the excited women and the awestruck disciples on the road to Emmaus that first day of the week. The doctrine of the Real Presence is less powerful than the image of the final meal in the upper room. None of the doctrines is less true than the stories. Indeed, they have the merit of being more precise, more carefully thought out, more ready for defense and explanation. But they are not where religion or religious faith starts, nor in truth where it ends.

Catholicism shares these stories with the other Christian churches. However, Catholicism invests the stories with its distinctive sensibility, developing Easter lilies and Santa Claus and the Feast of Corpus Christi.

Catholic devotions include, as I have said, Mary the mother of Jesus, angels and saints, souls in purgatory, statues, stained-glass windows, holy water, religious medals, candles. Most other Christian denominations do not engage in such devotions. Indeed, they dismiss them as superstition and perhaps idolatry. It is not my intention to defend Catholic devotional practices but rather to show that they illustrate how the Catholic religious imagination differs from the Protestant religious imagination. Since I will rely in this book on empirical data collected in the North Atlantic world, I will not attempt comparisons with other religious heritages—Islamic, Jewish, and Orthodox, for example. My aim is to specify how the Catholic imaginative tradition differs from other versions of the Western Christian story.

The fundamental insight which guides this exploration comes from the work of David Tracy, especially his *Analogical Imagination*.[3] Tracy noted that the classic works of Catholic theologians and artists tend to emphasize the presence of God in the world, while the classic works of Protestant theologians tend to emphasize the absence of God from the world. The Catholic writers stress the nearness of God to His creation, the Protestant writers the distance between God and His creation; the Protestants emphasize the risk of superstition and idolatry, the Catholics the dangers of a creation in which God is only marginally present. Or, to put the matter in different terms, Catholics tend to accentuate the immanence of God, Protestants the transcendence of God. Tracy is consistently careful to insist that neither propensity is superior to the other, that both need each other, and, in my sociological terminology, the correlation between the two imaginations and their respective religious traditions is low level. Nonetheless, they *are* different one from another.

Much of my sociological work in the last decade and a half has been an attempt to see whether Tracy's theory can generate sociological hypotheses which can be tested against data about the behavior and attitudes of the Catholic population. So far it has not been necessary to accept the null hypothesis that there is no distinctively Catholic religious sensibility. In fact, quite the contrary.

Cognitive psychologists have recently begun to insist that metaphors—statements that one reality is like another reality—are the fundamental tools of human knowledge. We understand better and explain more adequately one reality to ourselves by comparing it to another reality which we already know. Thus, poor bemused and doomed Romeo, struggling to give meaning to his love for Juliet, tells himself and us that she is like the sun. He is asserting that she brings light and warmth and cheer to his life, just as the sun does. She is not a ball of exploding gas, of course. She is both like and unlike the sun. Marvin Turner suggests that the parable, a narrative form of the metaphor in which humans project a known story onto a hitherto unknown story so that they can better understand the latter, is a way of knowing what may actually have preceded language in the evolutionary process of *Homo sapiens*.[4]

The Catholic imagination in all its many manifestations (Tracy calls it "analogical") tends to emphasize the metaphorical nature of creation. The objects, events, and persons of ordinary existence hint at the nature of God and indeed make God in some fashion present to us. God is sufficiently like creation that creation not only tells us something about God but, by so doing, also makes God present among us. Everything in creation, from the exploding cosmos to the whirling, dancing, and utterly mysterious quantum particles, discloses something about God and, in so doing, brings God among us. The love of God for us, in perhaps the boldest of all metaphors (and one with which the Church has been perennially uneasy), is like the passionate love between man and woman. God lurks in aroused human love and reveals Himself to us (the two humans first of all) through it. Eventually, the Church came to see that human love was indeed a sacrament (a metaphor *par excellence*) which discloses God's grace and makes it present among us.

I use the word "lurk" advisedly. The Catholic imagination at its best senses that God is, to use Richard Wilber's phrase, the "Cheshire smile which sets us fearfully free." Like the beloved in the Song of Songs, God leaves all kinds of hints of Her presence, but slips away just at the moment we think we might have caught a glimpse of Her. At the same time, like the lover in the Song of Songs, God flits around the garden and peers in the latticework, hoping to catch sight of His beloved in all her naked beauty.

While I'm at it, allow me to make another semantic disclaimer. In this essay I use the words "analogy" and "metaphor" interchangeably. In fact there is a distinction which is philosophically important if not immediately germane to my purposes. When one says that God is love, meaning like human love only more powerful and passionate, one is using a metaphor. When one goes a step further and says that human love is an analogy for God, one says that there is a reality in God which human love is like and in which in some fashion human love participates. Can there be metaphorical discourse about God which is not analogical? I am inclined to think that there cannot, but this is not the place to argue the subject.

In the Protestant heritage, there is considerable reluctance to go so far as to equate human love with divine. Marriage, while good and holy, has never become a sacrament. If one says in this tradition that human sexual union is like the union between God and Her people, there is an immediate need to insist that God's passion is also very different from human passion. Thus, the Protestant imagination (Tracy calls it "dialectical") stresses the "unlike" dimension of a metaphor and is in fact uneasy with the idea of metaphor.

The Reformers, rightly upset about the prevalence of superstition among the peasant peoples of Europe, thought that the analogical imagination brought God too close to the world and was responsible for superstition. Indeed, the dialectical imagination, latent in the Catholic heritage all along, emerged powerfully with the Reformers precisely because it had not been taken seriously enough by Catholic leadership (though what the Church could have done about the peasant superstition in Europe is another question). Tracy quite properly insists that the dialectical imagination is a necessary corrective to the analogical imagination.

However, if analogy is rejected, it is hard to find any philosophical justification for a metaphor about God. If human love, for example, does not in any way participate in God's love and vice versa, what justification is there for the comparison between the two? Are not the loves totally different realities and the metaphor which says one is like the other nothing more than wordplay?

The distinguished Protestant theologian Paul Tillich, displeased by the anthropomorphic language predicated of God, tried to sweep it away by talking about a God beyond God, about whom nothing at all could be said or known except negatively.

All God talk then is not only metaphorical but also idolatrous. We must live out our lives knowing that there is God but knowing nothing about God.

These philosophical and theological differences are the bases (or perhaps only the justifications and rationalizations) for the two different ways of approaching the divine reality that arose out of the Reformation. Put more simply, the Catholic imagination loves metaphors; Catholicism is a verdant rainforest of metaphors. The Protestant imagination distrusts metaphors; it tends to be a desert of metaphors. Catholicism stresses the "like" of any comparison (human passion is like divine passion), while Protestantism, when it is willing to use metaphors (and it must if it is to talk about God at all), stresses the unlike.

In my courses at the University of Chicago and the University of Arizona, students resist strongly the notion that human passion discloses God's passion. Human sexual love, they tell me, is lewd or lustful, while God's love is pure. Catholics are as likely to make this argument as are students from other denominations. The propensity to protect God from profanation, at the heart of the dialectical imagination, is very strong even among Catholics because official Catholicism has yet to make up its mind whether it really believes that sexual passion is not in itself lewd or lustful.

A metaphor is a two-way street. (The words "metaphor," "sacrament," "mystery," and "symbol" can be used interchangeably in this context, though in other contexts nuances and refinements might be necessary.) Romeo knows more about Juliet because he has been able to compare her to the sun, but in the act of making that comparison he also takes notice of the sun in a way which he had not before. Had he lived longer, he would often have pictured not only his lover as sunlight but also the sunlight as possessing some of the qualities of Juliet.

Similarly, in the sacramental comparison of human love with divine love, the passionate man and woman understand God better as they grasp that God loves like they do, only more so. But the participation of both loves in one another through the metaphor also enlightens the man and woman about their own love and the need especially for forgiveness and mercy in that love. The Catholic religious sensibility is often almost overwhelmed by the thickness of the metaphors in its dense forest of imagery and story. God and grace lurk everywhere. In the dictum "grace is everywhere" the emphasis can be placed on any of the three words. I suspect that for the creative artist possessed by the Catholic imagination, the emphasis is on the third.

Where did this forest come from?

Of all the world religions which emerged in the last half of the millennium before the Common Era and the first half of the first millennium of the Common Era, Catholicism is the most at ease with creation. It has never been afraid (at least not in principle) of "contaminating" the purity of spirit with sensible and often sensual imagery. On the face of it, this compromise with nature religion is strange. All the other world religions and quasi religions (like Platonism) have abhorred the practices and images of nature religion as defilement of spirit. Catholicism, in its better moments, feels instinctively that nature does not defile spirit but reveals it.[5] Hence Catholicism (again, in its better moments) has not hesitated to make its own the practices, customs, and devotions of the nature religions wherever it has encountered them—never more systematically, thoroughly, or creatively than in Ireland.

Whence comes this confidence?

Perhaps it arose from the explosive joy of the early Church over its experience of the risen Jesus. In any case, it certainly existed at the time of Pope Gregory's famous message to Augustine of Canterbury. The latter worried about the pagan customs of the Angles. Might they be put to Christian use? Gregory replied

When Almighty God has brought you to our most reverend brother Bishop Augustine, tell him what I have decided after long deliberation about the English people, namely that the idol temples of that race should by no means be destroyed, but only the idols in them. Take holy water and sprinkle it in these shrines, build altars and place relics in them. For if the shrines are well built, it is essential that they should be changed from the worship of devils to the service of the true God. When this people see that their shrines are not destroyed they will be able to banish error from their hearts and be more ready to come to the places they are familiar with, but now recognizing and worshipping the true God. And because they are in the habit of slaughtering much cattle as sacrifices to devils, some solemnity ought to be given to them in exchange for this. So on the day of the dedication of the holy martyrs, whose relics are deposited there, let them make themselves huts from the branches of trees around the churches which have been converted out of shrines, and let them celebrate the solemnity with religious feasts. Do not let them sacrifice animals to the devil, but let them slaughter animals for their own food to the praise of God, and let them give thanks to the Giver of all things for His bountiful provision. Thus while some outward rejoicings are preserved, they will be able more easily to share in inward rejoicings. It is doubtless impossible to cut out everything at once from their stubborn minds just as the man who is attempting to climb to the highest place rises by steps and degrees and not by leaps.[6]

The message does not say it, but the missionaries to the Angles and the Saxons (and the Jutes, whom no one ever mentions) followed Gregory's model even to the extent of using the name of their spring festival for the Christian Passover festival. "Easter" comes from "Eastre," which was the feast of Eastren, the Anglo-Saxon goddess of the dawn (that is, the East) and of spring and new life (the cognate of Venus, Aphrodite, and Brigid). Three symbols which represented her fertility were lilies, rabbits, and eggs. It took a lot of religious courage to risk such adulteration of religion.

The early Irish Christians took matters one step further by clinging to a belief in reincarnation from their pagan past: some of them decided that Brigid was the mother of Jesus reincarnate and had actually nursed Him. Hence, when they said Brigid was the "Mary of the Gael" they meant the phrase literally, as far as it is wise to take anything an Irish person says literally.

It is hard to imagine Jewish or Islamic or Platonist or Hindu or Buddhist or Parsi missionaries (should there have been any in these world religions) taking such liberties with their heritage.

It can be argued that early Western Christianity during its first twelve hundred years had no option in the matter. In the chaos which enveloped Western Europe during the time of the invasions and the gradual collapse of the Roman civil order, the Church lacked the resources to do anything more than spread a veneer of Christianity over the resident pagan cultures save in the royal courts, the monasteries, and eventually the universities (from which sources come the little we know about the early Middle Ages). People were baptized, married, and buried in Catholic rites administered by often semiliterate, and usually married, clergy who frequently had no idea what the words or the ceremonies meant. To expropriate as much paganism as one could was merely to make a virtue of necessity. Still, Catholic Christianity did not hesitate in carrying out this perhaps foolhardy strategy. In one sense, the Reformation was a protest of a segment of the clerical elite and the newly emerging middle class against the continuation of paganism at a time when the Dark Ages had been definitely left behind.

Historian Stephen Ozment, no foe to Protestantism, remarks of the Reformation and the Counter Reformation that they were a "conservative campaign on the part of elite Christian clergy to subdue a surrounding native culture that had always been and preferred to remain semi-pagan . . . an attempt to impose on uneducated and reluctant men and women a Christian way of life utterly foreign to their own experiences and very much against their own desires." Having undercut traditional Catholic ritual and practice, he adds, the Reformation unloosed far worse superstitions, especially concerning witchcraft, that were among the horrors of European preliterate culture.

Perhaps the compromise with nature religion in which Catholicism engaged was for reasons of both theory and practical necessity. Yet there is nothing in the attitude of Pope Gregory that reveals any hint that baptizing the metaphors of paganism was merely a pragmatic decision. Grace was everywhere even then.

If the rainforest of metaphors, which Catholicism not only made its peace with but also patently celebrated, provided it with an enormous wealth of resources (and, I will argue, is why

Catholics remain Catholic), it also created problems from which Catholicism has never been freed—superstition, folk religion, idolatry. What, for example, about Our Lady of Guadalupe? Some Catholic historians will argue that devotion to her is a form of folk religion which has crossed the admittedly broad and permeable boundary between Catholicism and paganism. The original shrine in Spain (an image on a rock) was a baptized pagan sanctuary. While the Mexican devotion to this Lady wears a patina of Catholicism, the customs and beliefs associated with it are mostly superstitious. Indeed, the woman does not even hold the Babe in her arms; she is not even a Madonna.

Yet does she not assure the masses of Mexico that God loves them like a mother as well as like a father, that she is on their side when they resist poverty and oppression? Will not Mexican Americans tell you that she is not carrying the Babe because she is pregnant with Him and will soon bring Him to life even as she brings life to us? Is she not then an appropriate popular exercise of the Catholic religious sensibility?

One cannot say the same thing about the feast of the Bomfim in Brazil—the festival of Our Lord of the Happy Death, celebrated the first week of January in Salvador da Bahia on a day also designated locally as the feast of St. Jerome. One searches the first days of the universal Church calendar for either festival without success; indeed, one searches the madcap celebration (perhaps in defiance of death) for signs of Christianity. Clad in the white turbans and dresses seen in voodoo ceremonies, a band of black women, out of respect, sweeps the steps of the Catholic church in the center of town where the procession begins and the steps of another overlooking the Atlantic where it ends, also out of respect. In between, the festival consists of heavy beer drinking, loud musical rhythms, extroverted dancing, and the most blatant (if usually inoffensive) sexual innuendo that this Nordeamericano has ever seen. A harmless festival perhaps, a delightful festival, but hardly Christian.

After returning to the United States, I described this phenomenon in a lecture at Old St. Patrick's Church in Chicago. An elderly man with snow-white hair, a red face, and the gray suit and brown sweater which are required for an Irish countryman at a lecture, said to me in a rich Galway brogue, "Ah, now, Father, aren't you being too hard on your Brazilians? Sure weren't the Irish that way for the first thousand years and aren't some of us that way even now?"

Thus spoke the analogical imagination. Thus, too, spoke a loyal (if perhaps not altogether explicit) disciple of Gregory the Great who was willing to grant a people the right to grow into Catholicism step by step instead of by leaps, even if the steps took a thousand years!

However, those who are possessed by the Catholic sensibility should realize the direction in which its risks lie.

Besides, the sexual innuendo in my Brazilian experience has never been quite that explicit in Ireland. Not in contemporary Ireland, anyway.

More's the pity?

Maybe.

Lest my intent be misunderstood, it may be useful to specify precisely what the book is *not* about.

1. I am not attempting a detailed and comprehensive statement of Catholic doctrine. Doctrine is the cognitive superstructure of a religious heritage and is essential. My goal, however, is to describe the imaginative and narrative infrastructure of the Catholic heritage, the experiences, images, rituals, and stories which are at the center of Catholicism and which influence Catholic behavior beyond the walls of the Church.

2. Nor will I strive to present the essential truths of Catholic belief, a worthy activity but one beyond the scope of this book. I am not trying to enhance the propositional faith of Catholics; my effort is to explain to Catholics and others how these experiences, images, rituals, and stories so tenaciously cling to Catholics and bind most of them to their heritage regardless of how far away from the Church they may move.

3. I have no intention of defending policies of the institutional Church. Thus, when I write about erotic desire, I must not be understood as endorsing (or disapproving of) the present policy of Catholic institutional leadership on contraception. Nor in my discussion of Mary the mother of Jesus as a metaphor for (or sacrament of) the Mother Love of God (that is, the immense fertility of God's passionate love for us) will I be defending the abuse of the Mary metaphor when it is converted into a negative sexual stereotype.[7]

4. I will not assert that the Catholic imaginative tradition—the way Catholics picture the world and God's relationship to it—is better than other ways which might be available but merely that it is different. Nor will I suggest that it is without potential weaknesses and flaws, especially its propensity for folk religion, superstition, and magic. Instead, I will suggest that it chooses to emphasize the presence of God in the world and runs

the risks of that choice while acknowledging that the opposite choice—to emphasize the absence of God from creation—has risks of its own.

5. I will not try to persuade the reader that the organized Church has always understood the best instincts of the Catholic imaginative heritage. As we have seen, at one time the institution, in the person of Pope Gregory the Great, urged Augustine of Canterbury to adapt Catholicism to the customs of the pagan Anglo-Saxons. In Ireland, the monks and missionaries appropriated everything they could from Irish paganism. Later, the same institution approved, though just barely, the efforts of Cyril and Methodius to adjust to Slavic culture. Still later, the institution destroyed the efforts of the Jesuits to do the same thing in China and India and Ethiopia with tragic results. It is by no means clear today that the institution, despite all its talk of enculturation, is prepared to take African culture seriously. The Church has always believed in some fashion that the sexual union is sacramental, an image of the union between Jesus and the Church, yet it has never quite been able to overcome the impulse to feel that sex is something shameful. Moreover, the Catholic instinct to believe that all space is sacred (sacramental) and that some spaces are more sacred than others has produced some of the most beautiful buildings in the world, but in contemporary America Catholics have often built churches which look like hangers for 747s or small-scale versions of Michael Jordan's United Center.

6. I do not intend to defend the institution from charges about its evil behavior—pogroms, the Crusades, the sack of Byzantium, the Spanish Inquisition, missionary imposition of Western culture on non-Western peoples, Pius XII's alleged silence during the Holocaust, to name a few obvious examples.

Made up of fallible and often ignorant and bigoted human be-ings, the institution has presided over unspeakable atrocities. I deplore and condemn such behavior. But in the present exercise my focus is on Catholic imagery, imagery to which the institu-tion has been utterly and perversely false when it violates basic human rights.

7. I do not propose that all Catholics are deeply affected by the Catholic imagination. Nor do I intend to imply that only Catholics have Catholic experiences about which to tell stories of one kind or another. Many Catholics act as if creation is God-forsaken, while many who are not Catholic act as if the whole of creation is sacramental and revelatory of God. I merely suggest that there is a propensity among Catholics to take the objects and events and persons of ordinary life as hints of what God is like, in which God somehow lurks, even if (as is perhaps often the case) they are not completely self-conscious about these per-ceptions of enchantment. I assert that there is a correlation—a modest one, as are all sociological correlations—between being a Catholic and being possessed by an enchanted imagination. On the other hand, I take it to be unlikely, though not absolutely im-possible, that a person who is not Catholic could be responsible for such monumental exercises of the Catholic sensibility as the Book of Kells, Notre Dame de Chartres, *The Divine Comedy*, "May Magnificat," or *Mean Streets*.

8. I do not propose to prove that there is a Catholic imagina-tion that is distinct from other religious imaginations but rather to illustrate the Catholic imagination with examples from the heritage and then to confirm with my own sociological work that predictions based on the assumption that there is a distinctive

Catholic imagination can be sustained by empirical data. In other words, in the language of social science, the null hypothesis that there is no such thing as a Catholic imagination need not be accepted.

9. This book is not an exhaustive description of the Catholic imagination. Perhaps one would not need to refer to all the books in the world (to borrow from St. John) to present such a work, but one would need many, many books. If I have left out your favorite examples of Catholic imagery, feel free to add or substitute them.

10. I am not claiming either virtue or deliberate intent for a Catholic artist or writer when I say his or her work displays a Catholic sensibility. When I say, for example, that Scorsese's *Mean Streets* is profoundly Catholic, it will not do to reply with stories about his marital problems. When I claim that *The Power and the Glory* is a profound Catholic novel about the sacrament of the priesthood, it would be inappropriate to reply with arguments about Greene and his mistress. To see God and creation through Catholic eyes it is not necessary to be a good Catholic, whatever that is. (Better to leave such judgments to God anyway!) Gounod probably realized that *Faust* was a profoundly Catholic opera. Verdi probably saw nothing especially Catholic about the sacrifice and redemption themes in *La Traviata*.

11. I do not mean that the Catholic sensibility is monolithic, that all its manifestations are fundamentally similar. Rather, because it is rooted in metaphorical "God talk" and because metaphors are polysemous, the Catholic religious imagination can disclose itself in many different forms. I will not focus on this

diversity in the present essay and thus will not attempt to discuss the variety of Catholic perspectives in such writers, for example, as Graham Greene, Georges Bernanos, J.F. Powers, Edwin O'Connor, Jon Hassler, and David Lodge. Nor will I deny the perverse and destructive elements in some manifestations of the tradition, such as those described so well by Michael Carroll in his *Madonnas That Maim*.

12. This, then, is not a book of theology but a book of sociology (albeit of a mostly nontechnical variety), a book of hypotheses tested against data. Many theologians assume (despite the frequent poverty of their own work) that, by the very fact that they are theologians, they are experts in the social sciences and have no need to attend to the logic and methods of those sciences. Since this book makes no theological assumptions and explicates no teachings about God (which is what theologians are supposed to do and which a few of them actually do at the present time), it must be critiqued on sociological and not theological grounds.

Finally, one point bears repeating: if there is a Catholic imagination there is perforce a Protestant imagination, and to write about one is not to oppose the other. As Tracy has said in season and out, both need one another; neither is superior to the other; indeed, they overlap. In a more unified Christianity, the necessary critique of one by the other may someday proceed more smoothly and gently. Yet they are different—not completely different, but somewhat different. I do not intend to attack the Protestant imagination when I show that ordinary Catholics are indeed possessed by a Catholic sensibility and that with regard to some social issues they are more socially concerned. The ultimate purpose of this essay is to explore a previously unexplored dimension of Catholicism and not to critique Protestantism.[8]

Catholics tend to see their churches as sacred places. Protestants do not. The baroque cathedral is not better than the auditorium, but it echoes with distinctly enchanted, and enchanting, voices.

== CHAPTER ONE ==

Sacred Place, Sacred Time

The autobahn from the Köln-Bonn airport approaches Köln from the East Bank of the Rhine. As one drives over the bridge one sees the skyline on the West Bank. It is not exactly Chicago as seen from the Shedd Aquarium (what is?), but it is still striking: the great spired Dom which dominates the city is surrounded, as by faithful servants, by seven Romanesque churches, each one representing a phase in the city's long history. Along the riverbank, picturesque multicolored buildings hint at a late medieval city. Gaily painted excursion boats and big barges with the flags of many countries move majestically in either direction. On the nearby railroad bridge, trains roar by at the rate of two per minute. If one has lived long enough, one remembers pictures of the devastated city immediately after the War in which the Dom, the victim of seventeen direct bomb hits, was a hollow shell surrounded by rubble. Once again, this historic city where the river meets the road has

OPPOSITE: The Dom at Köln. Photo by Reiner Gaertner, with permission.

Vertical

managed to survive, the Dom's pinnacles somehow invoking heaven's protection over the busy river traffic, the loud trains, the reconstructed waterfront, and the shops, office buildings, and hotels clustered along the bank of the Rhine. It had not protected the city or even itself from allied bombers, but it had presided over the post-war economic miracle. Its bells triumphantly celebrate its continued existence.

I shall discuss at some length Köln and its Dom because together they illustrate the key component of Catholic imagination—sacramentality, the presence of God in all creation. One cannot isolate the Dom from the history of the city. Köln is called "the holy city" not because its people are particularly virtuous but because it witnesses the presence of God lurking everywhere in creation.

I will then turn to a very different church which also tells of the presence of God in the world, but in a very different time and place—the mission of San Xavier del Bac in the Arizona desert south of Tucson.

In A.D. 48 the Emperor Claudius married Julia Agrippina, daughter of General Germanicus, who had been born in a town of the Ubii. She made the town a Roman city called Colonia Claudia Ara Agrippinensium, whence the name Cologne. It was not a bad place to live; an eighteen-kilometer aqueduct brought fresh drinking water into the city, and there was an underground drainage and sewage system. For four hundred years the city was the northeast cornerstone of the Roman Empire. When the German barbarians, by then Christian, drove the Romans away from the Rhine and occupied Köln, they built many churches[1] and appointed an archbishop who became one of the electors of the Holy Roman Empire, along with the archbishops of Mainz and Trier, the count palatine of the Rhine, the king of Bohemia, the elector of Brandenburg, and the elector of Saxony.

The Franks chose to make their capital at Aachen, or Aix-la-Chapelle, as it is also called. Then in A.D. 975 a Schottencloister was established, an Irish monastery, doubtless a major contribution to civilization, culture, and religion. One of the Romanesque churches near the Dom, Great St. Martin, may have been named after its first abbot.

For a couple of hundred years Köln was in eclipse. Then, when relative peace returned to what had once been the Roman Empire, its Shrine of the Magi became an important pilgrimage site. It even received the title "holy city" (*Heilige Stadt*), a title shared only with Rome and Constantinople. Albert the Great taught at the university, Thomas Aquinas was ordained in the Dom (the one beneath the present Dom), and Duns Scotus is buried in the Minorite (Franciscan) church.

Köln became a victim of all the religious wars in the sixteenth and seventeenth centuries and the Napoleonic wars after that. The whole of northwestern Germany was a burned-out battleground until after the Congress of Vienna. Then Köln underwent another one of its periodic revivals. It became a part of Prussia, a fact that Kölner Catholics, civilized by years of French occupation (though they hated the French) and accustomed to their relaxed Kölnsch Catholicism, didn't like at all. The city prospered until the Second World War, in part because it had a very progressive mayor, Konrad Adenauer, in the 1920s and 1930s.

He built parks, improved the university, and expanded business. He opened one of the first social science research centers in the world, for which ingenuity he deserves the highest of praises.

He became mayor again after the War until the British fired him, just as Hitler had done. The Americans intervened and reappointed him. He presided over the first steps in the rebuilding of the city, became the first Chancellor of the Bundesrepublic. Many give him the credit for restoring democracy to the German people.

With all this long and colorful—and tragic—history in mind, one ponders the gray gothic pile of the Dom and the scaffolding attached to various parts of it. The Kölners began to build their cathedral in A.D. 1248, at the height of the city's great prosperity, but they didn't finish it until the middle of the last century.[2] It seems an old and dirty building, though much of it is several centuries newer than Notre Dame de Paris, which somehow looks both more modest and more youthful. It is dark from pollution and its stone is crumbling. Yet the city cannot let it perish, not now and not ever. It is the fourth largest church in Europe, larger than any of the other medieval cathedrals. Not delicate by any means but impressive, awesome even, as it rears above the railroad station, the central plaza (renamed Roncalliplatz after Pope John XXIII), the Roman-German museum, and everything else in sight like a fiercely protective Roman-German mother.

It is indeed vast. Only St. Peter's in Vatican City, St. Paul's in London, and the cathedral in Santiago de Compostela are larger. Somehow its gothic arches make it seem even larger than the church in the Vatican. I should like to say that the misty light streaming through the windows create a glow that make one want to lose oneself in mystical contemplation. However, contemplation would have been about as easy as in the United Center before a Bulls' game or O'Hare International Airport at Christmas. The Dom is usually jammed with camera-clutching people of every hue under heaven, most of whom are barely aware that it is a sacred place or of what one ought to be doing there.

One wanders about indifferently, pausing to admire the astonishing collection of paintings, statues, altarpieces, tombs, and stained-glass windows. The place is a vast and striking museum, a reminder of a thousand years of history and art. Not exactly a church, but a special kind of Catholic sacred place.

The raison d'etre for the Dom and the city, the Shrine of the Magi, is the largest gilt reliquary in the West. It looks much like a golden Roman basilica, thought in fact it is three boxes, one on the top of the other two. Heaven forefend that each of the Magi would not have his own private tomb. The Magi themselves are carved in gold on the back panel along with Emperor Otto IV. Various apostles and prophets, all tall men who look like kings, are arranged on either side and on the front. Above it all, on what would have been the facade if it were truly a basilica, sits the King of Heaven looking down in approval at the whole scene. The shrine is covered with neatly arranged, multi-hued jewels. Emperor Otto IV had pillaged the precious stones from Byzantium and figured that they entitled him to a place near the three kings, observing them respectfully. The tomb of the Magi is a massive, overdone but sumptuous jewel box, 1.53 meters high, 2.2 meters long, and 1.1 meter wide and weighing approximately a ton.

The relics had belonged to the Dom in Milan for centuries. In 1164 Frederick Barbarosa confiscated them—"stole" would be a better word—and turned them over to his Chancellor for Italy, one Reinald von Dassel, who was also the archbishop of Köln. It's not hard to imagine Reinald saying to Frederick, "You owe

The Shrine of the Magi in the Dom at Köln. Photo by Reiner
Gaertner, with permission.

me a favor" and picking up his marker in the form of the relics. Seventeen years later, a certain Nicholas of Verdun established a workshop here to redo the reliquary. It was probably finished by 1225, a couple of decades before work started on the Dom. If the reliquary was designed to hold the remains of the Magi, so was the Dom built to hold the reliquary. Three million visitors come to the Dom every year, some days 40,000 pilgrims and tourists. They want to see the shrine even if they don't believe the legend.

In a corner of the Dom, one encounters the polychrome Madonna of Milan (another borrowing from the Italian city). The young woman, in robes of dark red, blue, and gold with a crown and a halo of stars, is lovely. Small wonder that the bare-chested (and crowned) Child reaches for her face with His right hand, while His left hand holds the world like a twelve-inch softball (in which we Chicagoans do not believe, taking it as only somewhat less than Gospel truth that a true softball is a sixteen-inch Chicago softball).

Köln is a city dense with religious history, pagan and then Christian, much of it acrimonious (for centuries the archbishop dared not live in the city) and some of it violent. The Alte Stadt (Old City) seems to have churches at almost every corner, most of them with colorful histories. Some, including the Dom, are built above pagan temples—often, like the Dom, above several layers of previous worship places. The city itself is arranged in a series of concentric rings radiating out from the remnants of the walls which once protected the heart of the city and the Dom. The outer rings are separated by parks or forests, a pattern which makes a charming and cosmopolitan (and very friendly) city all the more attractive. When the railroad came to Köln in the last

The Madonna of Milan. Photo by Reiner Gaertner, with permission.

century, the Kölners wanted it to circle the city in the same pattern and then go on to the north, but the Prussian-dominated government thought this was nonsense. With the same efficiency with which it launched two world wars, Berlin insisted that the Hauptbahnhof be constructed in the very center, right next to the Dom and a stone's throw from the Rhine. The noisy protests of the Kölners were ignored. Now, the locals admit ruefully that there is considerable charm in the juxtaposition of the old and the new, the sacred and the profane, the medieval and the modern. They will even concede that station is where it belongs. Besides, its location makes it easy for the tourists and pilgrims to find their way to the heart of historic Köln.

One might ask rather whether it was ever a Christian city, and whether there has ever been or indeed ever can be a city that honors the vision of the Gospels. In earlier eras, when the archbishop was in charge of the city and the institutional Church dominated its life and culture far more directly and explicitly than it does or wants to today, were the Gospel teachings any more influential on everyday behavior? The Shrine of the Magi, which attracted thousands of pilgrims to the city and was partially responsible for its importance for so many centuries, was stolen goods. So are the jewels on the shrine. The Karnival starts in Köln not the week before Ash Wednesday but on November 11, a date without religious significance to Catholics. There never was an age of faith anywhere and certainly not in Köln, only great works of art shaped by religious imagination, works which drew folk to God, often in spite of themselves. Unable to impose virtue on its members or to impart much religious education, the Church shaped faith by shaping imaginations. The resulting faith was limited, but not necessarily more so than is faith today.

Köln, then, is surely Catholic by heritage and tradition if not by religious devotion. Rhinelanders consider themselves to be more civilized than other Germans, and Kölners consider themselves to be more civilized than other Rhinelanders. Like the natives of all German-speaking countries, they regulate themselves with more rules than any other country in the North Atlantic world. Yet they are relaxed and friendly folk—the most friendly city in Germany, they will tell you, and not without reason—who approach life and its problems with a mixture of fatalism and humor not unlike that of the Irish.[3] They attribute this ethos to the fact that they are Kölnsch[4] Catholics, by which they are saying nothing about their loyalty to the papacy. One of my colleagues in the city told me that she had left the Church in 1988 (in anger at the pope) but that of course she was still and always would be a Kölnsch Catholic. She meant that she would always look at the world from the vantage point of one who lives in the shadow of the Dom.

I'm not celebrating this style of being Catholic. Like all styles of religious behavior, it has strengths and weaknesses. It may well be too casual, too indifferent, too relaxed, too tolerant of the weaknesses of human nature, too ready to accept the imperfections of the human condition. However, fanatical it is not, nor oppressive, nor narrow and rigid. Moreover, it is still Catholic if on its own terms, an approach that it now has in common with most of the Catholic world.

Is the Dom responsible for this religious style? Having come to know the city and its people pretty well, I suspect that in the absence of the Dom and what it stands for—and to make this point is the reason for my extended celebration of the city—Köln and the Kölners would be very different.

Catholicism has always believed (until recently, at any rate) that church buildings were important. If the whole of creation was sacred, if God was present in some fashion in all the objects, events, and persons of ordinary life, then there were some places which were especially sacred because God was present in them in a special way by virtue of the celebration of the Eucharist. From the very beginning of the Church's legal existence and its appropriation of unused basilicas (courthouses) in Rome, places of public worship assumed great importance, first on pragmatic grounds as houses enabling Christians to assemble, and then on aesthetic grounds as places to be made beautiful precisely because they were especially holy. It did not take very long for a theory to develop asserting that the beauty[5] of a sacred place made it a teacher of Christian truth and that the objects of beauty within it should tell the essential Christian stories to a mostly unlettered population.

Have the great Catholic churches of the world never been quiet, prayerful places where the faithful came to pray in reverent silence as a Gregorian chant floated in the background and incense wafted heavenward? If you want that sort of austere setting, you must go to a Benedictine abbey like that in the Brother Cadfael stories. The great Catholic churches of the world—whether Romanesque like Great St. Martin's, gothic like Chartres or Notre Dame de Paris, or baroque like St. Peter's in Rome, the Martinkirche in Bamberg (on the Jesuitinstrasse!), or the partially bombed out Jesuitinkirche in Mannheim—have always been crowded with people, tombs, chapels, altars, statues, shrines, altarpieces, paintings, tapestry, votive candles, and stained glass. They always have noisy bells which will keep you awake at night. The Dom in Köln is no more cluttered than St. Peter's or your local Italian parish church. Catholicism has tried to crowd all the metaphors from its forest inside its churches. The great cathedrals of Europe are in fact treasure houses of stories located inside of storied cities.[6]

At a time when both social conditions and technological limitations made it impossible to teach the faith by the book or by formal education, the church inundated its people with stories. In a time of widespread literacy when religion courses, textbooks, and how-to manuals can reach out to the whole population, the churches are still treasure houses of stories, save in some sterile modern churches with which architects and clergy, in a burst of mistaken ecumenism, have tried to placate the Protestant suspicion that Catholic churches hoard idols. A rule of thumb: if there are no votive candles in it, a church really isn't Catholic.

In the Catholic imaginative tradition churches overflow with stories, not only the central story of the Eucharist and the ongoing stories of the liturgical year (in which sacred place and sacred time combine), but many other stories, all of which tell of God's unremittingly merciful love. Even the Shrine of the Magi, with its dubious provenance and its blatant history of theft, tells of a birth in Bethlehem of Judah in the time of Caesar Augustus which brought hope to Jew and Gentile alike.

Some of the stories in the cathedrals flowed out into the city: the miracle and morality plays sprang out of the liturgical cycle at the altar, gathered force as performances inside the church during nonliturgical hours, and finally broke forth into the cathedral plaza as plays for the general populace. Similarly, the oratorios developed out of the polyphonic masses, gradually moved into the theaters, and eventually became operas. Very few Western artistic traditions were not shaped first in the churches. Ironically, the Catholic Church which presided over artistic works for so long and which let them develop freely beyond the church building has in the last couple of centuries lost interest in them, especially in this country.

What motivated the artists and benefactors who paid the artists? The desire to tell stories for the faithful, a wish to praise God with created beauty, the need for money to live, the artistic impulse for self-expression, the will to celebrate oneself?

How would it be possible to sort out these motives? And why should it be necessary? St. Peter's is no less stupendous, and the Pieta is no less a story of maternal grief, because the Borghese family has its name over the basilica entrance. Granted, by modern standards this obvious expression of patronage is a bit vulgar (and maybe the whole basilica is a bit vulgar), but there is no reason why the mixed motives that affect all human behavior should interfere with the stories being told.

But do we still need the stories that are being enacted, one way or another, all around us in such churches? Can't we leave alone the simple layperson who just wants to spend a few moments with her God in prayerful silence? Are there not enough catechisms, religion textbooks, theological monographs, papal encyclicals, and hierarchical statements that we no longer need to tell stories as much as we did during the preliterate epochs?

Only if our members are angels, creatures lacking in bodies. Stories are as important now as they ever were. Religion is story before it is anything else and after it is everything else. It is not necessary that all the story forms be maintained. It is possible that we can tell stories now more skillfully, more reverently, more effectively than we did in the past, though I wouldn't bet on it. But when a church ceases to be the center of events which bind together sacred time and sacred space through sacred narrative, it may be a very beautiful, dignified, reverent place, but it isn't Catholic anymore. When a church stops being a treasure house of stories, it stops being Catholic. Likewise, when even a simple church, like the wooden huts about which Gregory wrote to Augustine of Canterbury, is dense with stories, then it is surely Catholic. The more artistically skillful the church and professional the works of art which accompany the central narrative of the Eucharist, the better the storytelling and the more Catholic the church. The honoring of God and the passing on of the stories are tasks far too important to be done poorly. A Catholic church is a place where the rich stories of the Catholic heritage are told over and over again, with every skill that human ingenuity possesses. That is the reason for the Dom in Köln and the reason the city is called the *Heilige Stadt*. Without the city, no Dom. Without the Dom, no city.

The stories are also told in the mission church in Arizona which is called the "White Dove of the Desert" because it looms up from a great distance like a peaceful bird.

San Xavier—named after St. Francis Xavier, an early Jesuit follower of Ignatius of Loyola and a missionary in Asia—was the last mission station that Eusebio Kino founded on the trail north from Mexico. When the Jesuits were suppressed in the late 1800s, the mission was abandoned for a quarter century. Then, toward the end of the century, the Franciscans reestablished the mission, named after a Francis other than theirs. They built the present structure in the last decade of that century, and it has served the Tono Odham Native Americans ever since. It is the supreme artistic product of the mission trail, though, alas, it was built at the very end of the missionary thrust north from the center of New Spain and thus is a monument not to a new tradition but to one that had lost its energy.

The architecture of the mission is described as ultra-baroque or sometimes as late Hispano-Moorish baroque. The prefix "ultra" is appropriate. When one enters, the eyes are assaulted by a mass of dense, colorful, and exotic imagery. There are statues, paintings, frescoes, murals everywhere: not a space on the walls lacks an image, not a corner is free of niche and statue. One feels that one has entered a surrealistic world filled with saints—or, perhaps, is having a nightmare after reading a book about the saints. Indeed, angels and saints and the mother of Jesus are everywhere—watching, enchanting, inviting. After gasping in surprise, one becomes aware that these saints are not like the saints in one's own parish church. These saints are real people, handsome, attractive, each with a personality and a character of his or her own. "Who are these people?" one asks. Yes, of course, here is Santa Maria da Gloria, but she is no mere plaster statue of a woman. She is a real person. The artist who created her made her a full-bodied and full-blooded woman, an exercise in piety that exceeds even Bernini.

Only if one reads the guidebook available in the gift shop, or listens carefully to the taped lecture piped in over the public address system, does one perceive that there is a careful plan regulating the arrangements of the angels, the saints, and the mother of Jesus (of whom, it is alleged, there are one hundred and fifty images in the church). They are arranged hierarchically, with God and Jesus and Mary and St. Francis all fitting in their proper places and all telling us their own stories. Moreover, so we'll know that, though the church honors a Jesuit saint, the Franciscans built it and continue to staff it, the cord of the Franciscan habit circles the inner walls.

The parishioners have developed their own cycle of rituals and feasts to celebrate their saints, a mix of Catholic and Native American customs. While the result is certainly folk religion, it is substantially within the boundary that distinguishes Catholicism from paganism, though one could not imagine a sacred place or sacred time more different from those of the Kölner Dom. Yet both churches are treasure houses of stories, the same stories of a God who is deeply involved with His creation, but stories told with different accents and different dramatis personae. God is present both on the frequently overflowing banks of the Rhine and on the almost always dry banks of the Santa Cruz River.

In San Xavier one always returns to the compelling faces of the statues. We do not know who designed the White Dove of the Desert, nor do we know who made the statues. It seems unlikely that the natives sculpted them. Perhaps artisans from Mexico City deserve the credit. The faintly Semitic cast of the faces of many suggests that the artists may have been Sephardics (as they still call themselves), Jews who converted to Christianity lest they be expelled from Spain. However, while the images are similar to those in some baroque churches in Europe, the humanity of the icons is strikingly original. God, the saints in San Xavier seem to be telling us, lurks in the stories and in the faith of real people and not sub- or super-humans frozen in artifice.

Saints are important to Catholics because their lives are stories of God's love. Like the angels, they are sacraments of God's love, of God's immediate care for humans, and of the response of some humans to that love. God hides in the lives and the images of the saints. Hence Catholics are not ashamed of the saints. In some Catholic art, like Graham Greene's *The Power and the Glory*, Georges Bernanos's *Diary of a Country Priest* and *Under the Son of Satan*, Lars von Trier's *Breaking the Waves*, and Nancy Savoca's *Household Saints*, the question of the nature of sainthood is agonized over. The nameless whiskey priest is a coward in Greene's novel. Bernanos's two priests are clumsy dullards. The women in the two films (played by Emily Watson and Lili Taylor) seem to be simpleminded misfits and are arguably crazy. Bess is denied Christian burial by her church. A thoroughly modern nun-psychologist tells Teresa Santangelo's parents that the young woman is a victim of psychotic delusions and religious obsessions. Yet God vindicates all of them: the whiskey priest dies a martyr; Bernanos's priests both work miracles; bells peal in the sky in honor of Bess; and the garden in front of the mental institution where Teresa dies blooms overnight despite a snowstorm, and the scent of roses fills her death room.[7] Saints are perhaps a bit mad. God sometimes seems to display bad taste in the choice of His special loves. But there is no accounting for tastes when it comes to love. The stories of saints, which fill Catholic churches from Köln to the Sonoran desert and beyond, tell how magical human nature can become when it is filled with God's love.

The point need not be labored any further. Catholic churches (some more than others and some hardly at all) are strongholds of the analogical imagination, of stories of God's presence in the human condition. They cannot help themselves. If they're Catholic, they cannot be anything else.

But surely no claim can be made that these treasure houses of stories have an impact on Catholic behavior today?

In its 1993 General Social Survey, the National Opinion Research Center (NORC) included a module about culture.[8] The data collected made it possible to raise again the question of Catholics and the fine arts, a question which was debated in the 1950s and early 1960s. Might it be that the analogical imagination has an impact on Catholic involvement in the fine arts?

The question may seem absurd. While it presided over the fine arts for more than a millennium, the Church in its present Counter-Reformation modality could not care less about them. True, there are Catholics working in the fine arts both as performers and creators, but they are invisible Catholics who keep their religion to themselves and whose work is not, to all appearances, influenced by that religion. The Catholic elite which once lamented the lack of interest by Catholics in culture is now more concerned about ideological crusades of the left or the right. To the extent that the elites think at all about the subject of high culture, they picture suburban upper-middle-class Catholics as materialist, consumerist, secularist pagans who have little concern for the mind or the spirit, a position which corresponds to the Vatican's image of American Catholics—affluent couch potatoes who would rather watch a film on video than go to a theater. A similar image exists in the media and among the academic elite: Catholics are not interested in the fine arts and the fine arts are not interested in Catholics. Catholics are no longer seen as illiterate and anti-intellectual immigrants, but neither are they viewed as sophisticated enough and refined enough to enjoy high culture. Instead, they watch television every night.

Five types of fine arts patronage were addressed in the survey and are pertinent to the present investigation. Respondents were asked whether they enjoyed classical music or opera, and whether they had in the previous twelve months attended an art gallery show, an art museum exhibition, or a live performance of classical dance, classical music, or opera (excluding school performances).

Most would assume, I believe, that Catholics are less likely than Protestants to respond positively to these questions, or at least their responses would be no different from those of Protestants. My own expectation was the opposite: the analogical imagination would, I thought, lead to greater Catholic involvement. The stories that shout at Catholics in their churches, in the liturgy, and in the liturgical year will open them to the quieter but still powerful stories which are told outside of church.

My expectations were sustained.[9] Catholics were more inclined to say that they liked the opera (27 percent to 19 percent) and classical music (55 percent to 47 percent). They were also more likely to report attendance at a fine arts performance in the preceding year—24 percent to 15 percent for dance, 21 percent to 13 percent for music, and 47 percent to 35 percent for visual arts. Fifty-six percent of Catholics had attended at least one fine arts performance or exhibition in the previous year as opposed to 44 percent of the Protestants. Twenty-seven percent of Catholics attended two or more events, as did just 15 percent of the Protestants, and 10 percent of Catholics attended all three kinds of performances (dance, music, visual arts) compared to 5 percent of Protestants. All the differences are statistically significant.

How can this be so? Members of a Church whose one artistic interest not so long ago was censoring films and who are only a single generation removed from the immigrant neighborhoods of their heritages, how can it be that American Catholics today rank substantially above the national average in their demonstrated interest in the fine arts?

First of all, one must consider the possibility that this surprising finding might be the result of demographic and social factors. I elected to investigate further the greater Catholic propensity to leave the couch for the opera house, the concert hall, and the art gallery. Such variables as age, gender, race, city size, region, education, and income reduce the correlation between Catholics and fine arts attendance by 36 percent, with education and city size being the most powerful predictors. Catholics are in part more likely to attend fine arts performances because they are better educated than Protestants and because they live in large cities where more such opportunities are available. Still, the majority of the difference in fine arts participation between Catholics and Protestants remained constant irrespective of these factors.

My theory led me to wonder whether Catholic church attendance, steeped as it is in a sacramental or metaphorical context, would have a special impact on fine arts consumption. If one is surrounded by cultural artifacts (however weakened and compromised) when one worships, one might perhaps also have a greater interest in the fine arts. Frequency of churchgoing correlates dramatically with Catholic fine arts attendance and does not correlate significantly with Protestant fine arts attendance. The largest difference between Catholic and Protestant fine arts attendance is concentrated precisely among the regular churchgoers. Indeed, the interaction between Catholics and church attendance eliminates the difference between Catholics and Protestants.

Some readers will doubtless say that they are not surprised by the fact that Catholics have caught up to and surpassed the rest of the country in interest in the fine arts. But I challenge anyone to say that they are not surprised by the fact that it is the regular Sunday (or Saturday afternoon) Catholics who are most likely to be interested in the fine arts.

Can I demonstrate that this phenomenon is linked to a distinctively Catholic imagination? In my work on narrative religion I have developed a four-item scale, which I call the Grace Scale, that measures a respondent's image of God as mother versus father, lover versus judge, spouse versus master, and friend versus king. I discuss the development, rationale, and predictive power of the scale at great length in *Religion as Poetry* and will not repeat the discussion here. Catholics, as one would expect from Tracy's theory, score higher on the scale than do other Americans. In the present context, the question arises of whether this scale also influences Catholic fine arts participation. Indeed, a graceful image of God does affect attendance at artistic productions, but only for Catholics. For Protestants there is a (nonsignificant) negative correlation between the Grace Scale and the fine arts; for Catholics there is strong and positive correlation. The difference between Catholics and Protestants in fine arts participation is concentrated among those who have high scores on the Grace Scale. Not only is there a link for Catholics between church attendance and the fine arts but there is also a link between religious imagery (that is, views of God) and the fine arts.

A third link in the chain might be the establishment of a stronger relationship among Catholics between religious imagery and church attendance. Should such a link be established, one could well call the emerging model an example of the liturgical imagination. There is strong evidence of the existence of such a link. There is a negative correlation for Protestants between religious imagery and frequent church attendance and a positive link for Catholics. Catholics with high scores on the Grace Scale are more likely to go to church; conversely, Protestants with a low score are more likely to go to church. Or, to put it perhaps more plausibly, frequent church attendance for Catholics enhances their gracious religious imagery and for Protestants frequent attendance diminishes such imagery.

Thus the following model emerges:

1. Catholics are more interested in the fine arts than Protestants, and those Catholics who go to church regularly are the most likely to be interested in the fine arts.

2. Catholics are more interested in the fine arts because they have more graceful images of God, and those Catholics who have the most graceful image of God are the most likely to be interested in the fine arts.

3. Among Catholics the correlation between graceful imagery and regular churchgoing is positive. Among Protestants it is negative.

To test this model, I applied standard mathematical formulas employed in the social sciences and found that a liturgical imagination, a mix of church attendance and graceful images of God, does indeed account in part for the higher rate of fine arts behavior among Catholics.[10] Liturgy and the fine arts are linked—a notion which would have been taken to be obvious and beyond debate from Constantine to the Council of Trent.

The findings are statistically significant; the fitted model is robust. Yet the logic of the argument is delicate. The assumption that religion is story (narrative image) before it is anything else and after it is everything else is strange, and the findings may seem odd, even bizarre, to some readers. Who would have thought that Catholics had passed the national averages in interest in the fine arts and that there is a link between religious images, church attendance, and the fine arts, though only among Catholics? Admittedly, the complexity of the model does not respond to the need for sweeping generalizations about the laity, which generalizations are so beloved by theologians, religious educators, liturgists, parish priests, and the pope.

The model may be acceptable statistically because it fits the data, but it is also likely to be unacceptable existentially because it does not fit the perceptual structures of many Catholic leaders and teachers. In defense of its complexity, I would respond that reality is complex; only cautious and nuanced generalizations can possibly be accurate. I hope that some readers will ponder that truth and reflect carefully on my model of the liturgical imagination before they dismiss it out of hand.

The focus of this analysis was to account for the greater level of interest in the fine arts among American Catholics. But the important conclusion of the analysis is that Catholic interest in the fine arts reveals a mostly preconscious dynamism—a liturgical imagination linking graceful stories of God and church attendance—at the core of the Catholic religious heritage. There appears to be a distinctive and very powerful liturgical spirituality among Catholics. This mostly unperceived liturgical spirituality merits further reflection as a resource for, and challenge to, Catholic leaders. More theologically, it is a spirituality which reflects the nearness of the Spirit, a present and not distant Spirit, an analogical and not dialectical Spirit, among the Catholic laity.

This liturgical spirituality suggests that the assumption that the laity are Spirit-less is both arrogant and ignorant.

By "liturgy" here I do not mean "the Liturgy" in the ordinary Catholic sense. Nothing could be more destructive of the liturgical imagination then what passes for Liturgy in many American parishes: weekly doses of precious theorizing, cute tricks, inarticulate commentators, semiliterate readers, drab music, and poor homilies, and the multiplication of noncanonical (and hence illegal) rules by various gatekeepers ("liturgists," religious educators, RCIA directors). If the liturgical imagination continues to survive, it will do so despite the "liturgists" and not because of them. Its strength is rooted in the depths of the Catholic psyche with its ability to sense grace lurking everywhere.

Astonishingly, then, the ordinary weekend Eucharist in the ordinary Catholic church does have an impact on the imaginations of Catholics and on one unexpected measure of behavior beyond the church building. It may and probably does affect many other kinds of behavior, too, but fine arts participation is one that is intimately related to the imagination. Catholics may be especially addicted to fine arts storytelling because their lives have been shaped by so much storytelling since their first conscious moments. However imperfect the story told, however inartistic its rendering, however unimaginative its exercise of the Catholic imagination, this storytelling still works. Here, finally, is empirical validation of the policy decision that St. Gregory made a millennium and a half ago and evidence of the continuity between the Kölner Dom and the ordinary parish church.

Not only is the Dom—along with all the other Catholic churches in the world—a sacred place, a treasure house of stories, but it is also a theater in which sacred time is celebrated. Catholic churches are for festivals. Consider the story of one festival:

> I should like to have a great ale-feast for the King of Kings; I
>   should like the Heavenly Host to be drinking for all eternity.
> I should like to have the fruits of Faith, of pure devotion;
> I should like to have the seats of Repentance in my house.
> I should like to have the men of Heaven in my own dwelling; I
>   should like the tubs of Long-Suffering to be at their service.
> I should like to have the vessels of Charity to dispense; I
>   should like to have the pitchers of Mercy for their
>   company.
> I should like there to be Hospitality for their sake. I should
>   like Jesus to be here always.
> I should like to have the Three Marys of Glorious renown,
> I should like to have the Heavenly Host from every side.
> I should like to be rent-payer to the Lord. He to whom He
>   gives a good blessing has done well in suffering distress.

Even by the standards of the Irish, an outrageous people, this tenth-century scene is outrageous: God present at a drinking feast, an Irish warrior king striding in from the rain with a great thirst and expecting a great party.

Hilaire Belloc's famous verse is more bombastic and less subtle than those of Micheal O'Siadhail:

> Where'r the Catholic sun does shine
> There's music and laughter and good red wine
> At least I've found it so,
> Benedicamus Domino.

Catholics love festivals, which is to say, they love parties, especially those which mark turning points—any kind of turning point, and no Catholic group loves them more than Mexicans. Ask a Mexican American student about the content of her religion, and she will tell you about the parties and the celebrations; push her for substantive content, and she'll show you a calendar issued by Tucson's El Charro restaurant with a saint's name for every day in the year—far more than the calendar of the Universal Church contains. Everyone, it seems, has at least three names, and a compadre and a commadre for each name. You need the calendar at hand to remind yourself of the parties for your spiritual children.

"Yes," you say, if you are an Anglo-Saxon Celt (and interested in prosaic religion), "but what does it all mean?" Baffled, the latina will finally respond, "Well, I suppose it means that we love our families and celebrate with them whenever we can, and that we know God comes and celebrates with us."

Once a student said, "If we really want to be good Catholics, we're going to have to learn the rules like you Irish do. That's why we send our children to Catholic schools." Whoever wrote the poem about the great pool of ale back in the tenth century would not, I think, be amused.

Robert Orsi, in his classic book about Italian street festivals, argues that they are not mere exercises of superstition but rather celebrations of Italian community and family culture during the difficult process of becoming American and continuing to be Italian. The Irish clergy at the chancery "downtown" underestimated the importance of these celebrations to the religion of the immigrants and their children; they misunderstood the festivals' deeply religious nature. In the *Godfather* films, the festivals are depicted for what Orsi says they are, religious celebrations. On the other hand, Michael, the loan shark in *Mean Streets* comments that those "fucking festivals get in the way of everything."

That Catholicism is a religion of festival hardly need be proven. Witness the changing liturgical year, with its different-colored vestments and its different themes, and special festivals like All Saints and All Souls (which go back to Celtic antiquity), the midnight Mass at Christmas, the washing of feet on Holy Thursday, the reading of the Passion on Good Friday, the Easter Vigil with its fire and water, First Communions, May crownings, grammar school graduation, Mary Day at harvest time, Irish wakes. The festivals are so much a part of the life of Catholics that they notice them only when they're away from home, in a place where there are no such festivals. If religion is truly good news, then there really should be a celebration, and probably a party.

Until the last century, the Irish used to make love in the fields outside a house where there was a wake and thus asserted that life was stronger than death.

It is arguable that the festival as a point in sacred time is less important to Catholics today than it was in the peasant past. We Celtic Catholics no longer dance by the lakes at springtime as we once did (and did St. Joan of Arc). Or maybe we do, but at country clubs and with no sense of the religious implications of such spring fertility rites; more's the pity. Yet we still have festivals and liturgical seasons and big celebrations, so the resource remains for those who understand how important feasts still are in the rhythms of human life.

David Lodge, in his wondrous novel *Therapy*, celebrates the pilgrimage of his protagonist to the Festival of Santiago de Compostela, a pilgrimage which, together with reading Kirkegaard, heals the man's soul. Combining the two imaginations, analogical and dialectical,[11] in the same "therapy" is a deft touch, evidence that the two imaginations need not exclude one another. It is also an object lesson to those contemporary Catholic ideologues who wish to strip all festival from the liturgy and to eliminate all devotions (including festivals) save the Eucharist.

Gregorian chant, long since dismissed by those ideologues as "irrelevant," has suddenly become popular because of the work of the monks of Santo Domingo de Silos—and now many more monastic communities following in their footsteps. Chant, however, is not simply the "easy listening" music it is currently being marketed as. It is musical prayer which marks the ebb and flow of the seasons and the festivals, an ebb and flow which even at the middle of the present century shaped the religious life of the seminary I attended. (Chant was probably the only truly excellent thing which occurred at that seminary.) Thus, when one heard *"Rorate Coeli desuper et nubes pluant justum!"* from the *Scola Cantorum*, one knew it was Advent and could almost taste Christmas. The *Plange Lingua* told us it was Holy Thursday, *Haec Dies Qualm Fecit Dominus* meant it was Christmas, and the *Exultet Jam Angelica Turbus Caelorum* signaled the dawn of Easter. That music is gone now, or practically gone, but it stood for the Catholic sense that there should be sacred times and sacred festivals and sacred celebrations.

This sense may be attenuated now but it persists. There are still May crownings and priests still wear different-colored vestments at different times of the year.

The link between frequency of church attendance and fine arts participation described earlier in this chapter also proves that a dimension of sacred time is linked to the Catholic imagination. Can

I provide specific evidence that Catholics still have a sense of festival? As far as I can discover no survey ever carried out asks questions about festivals and feasts, which may be a result of the fact that Catholics have only recently come to the survey profession.

Data are available, however, which measure sociability, a kind of first cousin to festivity. The General Social Survey asked:

> Would you use this card and tell me which answer comes closest to how often you do the following things:
>
> Spend a social evening with relatives
>
> Spend a social evening with someone who lives in your neighborhood
>
> Spend a social evening with friends who live outside the neighborhood
>
> Go to a bar or tavern
>
> Spend a social evening with your parents
>
> Spend a social evening with your brother or sister

The possible answers were: Almost every day, once or twice a week, several times a month, about once a month, several times a year, about once a year, never.

The responses clustered into two patterns, one emphasizing relatives, parents, and siblings, the other neighbors, friends, and bars. There was no difference between Catholics and others in socializing with relatives, but Catholics were significantly more likely than everyone else to socialize with neighbors and friends and at bars. More than a third of Catholics visited a bar once a month, as opposed to less than a fifth of Protestants. The difference in sociability among Catholics hints at greater interest in festivals.

Another first cousin to festivity is leisure. Catholics are significantly more likely than Protestants (though only just barely) to say that, if they had the chance, they would like to arrange for more leisure in life. This propensity also correlates positively with church attendance for Catholics. Frequent church attendance inclines Catholics to value leisure more highly, but it has no such impact on Protestants. Again, in the absence of direct evidence, the finding only hints indirectly at the persistence of festival in the Catholic experience. However, if one did not have in mind the paradigm of Catholic festivity, one would not have looked at either sociability or leisure.

The Catholic imagination, then, revels in stories that are festivals and festivals that are stories. The church, whether cathedral or parish, is not the only place where these stories of God's love incarnated in space and time are told. But it is the place where the story treasures are stored and out of which they flow.

CHAPTER TWO

Sacred Desire

Erotic desire has on occasion been portrayed in art with a Catholic perspective.[1] Moreover, on occasion it has been considered sacramental in the Catholic heritage, so sacramental indeed that the union born of erotic desire has become an official sacrament of the Church. In principle, if sexual attraction is part of the human condition, if it has been created by God, however indirectly, and if human nature, however flawed, is still fundamentally good, and finally if sexual imagery is used both in the Jewish and the Christian scriptures as a metaphor for God's love, how can one possibly deny its sacramental value?

From what we now know of the evolutionary process, it selected in our species for males and females with a propensity to bond for sustained periods of time, a propensity based on affective desire between the male and the female. The offspring of such quasi-bonded couples had a better chance of surviving into

OPPOSITE: Bernini's St. Teresa in divine ecstasy. Courtesy CORBIS/Bettmann.

adulthood than the offspring of other couples; hence, they shaped the future development of the species.

Proto-love was a necessary prelude to the emergence of *Homo sapiens*. Once the capacity for tenderness toward the mate appeared, it developed in some members of the species into a capacity for tenderness toward others—relatives, friends, neighbors, and, of course, children; the members of the species gifted with the genes that passed on such a capacity were again most likely to protect their children into adulthood. Without erotic desire, now transformed into a much broader tenderness, humankind could not have developed into what it is today.

There is nothing in this brief summary that the Catholic tradition cannot accept. Catholics believe that human nature is good; that God designed the human reproductive process and that it is also good; and that human love between man and woman is a sacrament, a hint, a revelation, a sign, a metaphor for Jesus' love for His Church and for God's love for His people.

Nor do Catholics have any trouble with the social science finding that sexual desire between the man and woman leads them into marriage, helps to heal the wounds and frictions of daily life, and often draws them together in a renewal of their love. When the scholars who study those who came before us in the evolutionary process report that this erotic attraction existed even before the species became fully human and was a necessary prelude to the emergence of humankind, Catholics are hardly inclined to be offended or to want to debate their finding. Was it not clever of God, they might say, to arrange such an ingenious process? The audience talks Pope John Paul II gave on human sexuality early in his pastorate in effect confirmed such a view of erotic desire as good, virtuous, beautiful, and sacramental.

The most obvious and powerful evidence of the goodness of erotic desire is the presence in Scripture of the Song of Songs, an intensely erotic series of poems about the passion between two young people who are patently not married. Even in the frequently bowdlerized contemporary translations, the desire of the two for one another is obvious. Attempts to spiritualize their emotions, or to divert their desires into a figurative translation, do not finally work. Curiously, many if not most Catholics are unaware of the Song (or of the love story in the book of Tobit). Catholic teachers and clergy apparently are afraid that the Song will confuse the laity with dirty thoughts.

In theory Catholicism says that sex is good, but in practice the Church has yet to shake the Platonist notion that sex is dirty. Hence the Church's fear of erotic imagery. Even when the imagery is blatant, as in the case of the plunging of the candle into the water at the Easter Vigil, the Church tries to pretend that the erotic dimension is not there. So the Latin words which ask that the candle fructify the water (the candle is the male element, the water the female; the candle is Jesus, the water the Church; we who are baptized with the water are the firstfruits of this passionate union) have been replaced by a weak prayer that the candle "visit" the water; and it is not required that the priest actually plunge the candle into the water. How puritanical can you get!

Consider Bernini's statue of St. Teresa being transfixed by the arrow of divine love. It dares to portray her ecstasy as orgasmic, as explicit a metaphor as one could imagine. The saint herself was not hesitant about the use of erotic vocabulary in her description of her relationship with God. The lover poetry of her confrere, San Juan de la Cruz, is intensely erotic. Consider his poem "One Dark Night Fired with Love's Urgent Longings,"

Rubens's *Bathsheba at the Fountain*. Courtesy the Dresden National Art Museum.

written perhaps when he was imprisoned, starved, and tortured by fellow Carmelites:

1. One dark night,
fired with love's urgent longings
—ah, the sheer grace!—
I went out unseen,
my house being now all stilled.

2. In darkness, and secure,
by the secret ladder, disguised,
—ah, the sheer grace!—
in darkness and concealment,
my house being now all stilled.

3. On that glad night,
in secret, for no one saw me,
nor did I look at anything,
with no other light or guide
than the one that burned in my heart.

4. This guided me
more surely than the light of noon
to where he was awaiting me
—him I knew so well—
there in a place where no one appeared.

5. O guiding night!
O night more lovely than the dawn!
O night that has united
the Lover with his beloved,
transforming the beloved in her Lover.

6. Upon my flowering breast
which I kept wholly for him alone,

there he lay sleeping,
and I caressing him
there in a breeze from the fanning cedars.

7. When the breeze blew from the turret,
as I parted his hair,
it wounded my neck
with its gentle hand,
suspending all my senses.

8. I abandoned and forgot myself,
laying my face on my Beloved;
all things ceased; I went out from myself,
leaving my cares
forgotten among the lilies.[2]

If one reads those verses without knowing who the author is or what he is talking about, but merely accepts them at their face value, they are clearly about a man sneaking out of his house under cover of darkness in search of a night of pleasure with his human lover. Indeed, the poem is not unlikely to stir up erotic feelings among readers if they consider only the text and not the context. Catholic prudes will scream that one ought not to take the poem out of its proper context. However, the imposition of a context on a work of art which is not immediately evident from the text itself is an abuse of the work. St. John of the Cross presumably knew very well what he was doing when he compared a human assignation to an assignation with God. If a nighttime union of lovers is evil in itself (or, as St. Augustine would have it, evil if done for any purpose other than conceiving children), then it would be the worst kind of blasphemy to compare it to an assignation in the dark of night with God.

St. John is clearly referring back to the erotic verses of the Song of Songs. But it will not do to try to write off that Song as allegorical, especially now that Scripture scholars are virtually unanimous in the conclusion that the Song is a collection of erotic love poems. St. John is using human passion as a metaphor for divine passion—a thoroughly Catholic metaphor, however much it may offend some Catholics. The metaphor runs so consistently through both Jewish and Christian Scriptures that it is extremely difficult to exclude or ignore. Yet the temptation to allegorize it out of existence remains strong.

Marital liturgies have never hesitated to compare human love with divine love. The Sarum ritual includes a blessing of the marriage bed and a prayer that the bride may be compliant and vigorous in bed. These elements were eliminated when the Sarum rite was introduced into the Book of Common Prayer. Lay Catholic writers such as Dante, von Eschenbach, and especially Chaucer did not hesitate to use erotic desire as a component of their work.

In this dimension of the Catholic tradition there is no question that erotic desire is part of human life and an important part at that. Like all powerful human energies, it can turn demonic, but it is not evil in itself.

Yet another element of the Catholic tradition, influenced by St. Augustine and the neo-Platonic tradition, comes close to asserting that desire is evil, immoral, sinful. Desire deprives humankind of its rationality and reduces it to the level of the beasts; sexual pleasure is sinful unless its purpose is the conception of children; women are whitened sepulchres because they lead men into sin. Humankind should try to avoid erotic need, yield to it as rarely as possible, pretend as best it can that erotic desire does not exist, and speak of sex only in hushed whispers.

It is hard to argue against this perspective whether it is defended in the elevated prose of personalist asceticism or, as is more often the case, in the viciousness of outraged private sensibility. It is a position that is beyond discussion, self-evidently correct, and supposedly the only truly Catholic attitude toward sex. Statues of the mother of Jesus ought not to have breasts; neither should those of any other women saints; Michelangelo's figures require loincloths; sex ought not to be mentioned in polite conversation; the fact that men and women find one another's bodies attractive and often passionately desire those bodies ought to be hidden as completely as possible; sex should be kept a secret from children; there is no possible use for eroticism in Catholic art.

That settles that!

The fury with which this viewpoint is defended, a fury comparable to the worst anti-erotic manifestations of Puritanism, suggests that the defenders have problems with their own sexuality. Their inability even to listen to any other position, much less to perceive that another position is compatible with the Catholic heritage, confirms this suspicion. Sex is dirty and that is that.

A few of the Catholic puritans (and there were Catholic puritans long before there were Puritans) argue that the borderland between the erotic and the pornographic is so narrow and so dubious that the erotic must be avoided lest it either become or, worse, be perceived as pornographic. In fact, however, the border is wide and the erotic and the pornographic are easily distinguished from one another by those who do not have prurient minds.

Thus, a woman who views Bernini's St. Teresa and understands what the artist is doing will surely recall her own orgasmic
experiences and recognize what the metaphor implies. Moreover, she may find herself in the beginnings of sexual arousal and
yearn for another orgasmic experience. Whether her husband
will be sensitive enough to the artist's designs to recognize the
similarity between the saint's expression and his memory of his
wife's expression may be less certain, because men are often less
perceptive in these matters than women. If he does, it is possible
that he too will feel the beginnings of sexual arousal.

The point here is not that the none-too-subtle metaphor embodied in the statue will always or even often lead to sexual
arousal. Most likely it will do so only rarely. The point is rather
that the metaphor has the capacity to do so for those who are
sensitive to its implications. Moreover, for those who are open to
the metaphor in the statue, the link between divine and human
penetration may add an extra dimension to the observer's understanding of erotic desire.

In our fable of the husband and wife who are both aroused by
the statue and who later make love because of it (perhaps without
mentioning to one another the impetus for this particular
episode), it is possible that the encounter will be a richer one because of this source of inspiration and contribute in some small
way to the enhancement of their ongoing love affair.

Again, I make no claim that such an outcome is inevitable or
even likely, only that it is possible. Nor do I claim that such an
outcome existed in the mind of the sculptor, only that he was
very well aware of the metaphor involved in his work. As he fashioned the ecstatically pleasured face of the saint, did Bernini experience desire for the body of whomever was his bedmate at the

Bernini's *Ecstasy of St. Theresa*. Courtesy CORBIS.

time? I wonder how it would have been possible for him not to do so, especially given the fact that for mature men the fulfillment of a beloved woman is even more important than their own fulfillment.

Most Catholic puritans, hearing this reflection on Bernini's statue, would want promptly to hide it somewhere. Any work of art that stirs up erotic need—and the joy which comes with it—should be covered up. As if one can walk along Michigan Avenue on a spring day and not experience sexual desire. Or sit on a beach. Or swim in a public pool.

The attitude that anything which incites erotic arousal is pornographic is simply unacceptable, as is the attitude that to use the word "breast" in a story, much less to describe the wonders of a particular breast, is ipso facto pornographic. Human secondary sexual characteristics have evolved in such a way that they serve two purposes. The female breast, for example, exists to nurse the young, but it takes the form and shape that it does to attract men. To say that men tend to be obsessed with women's breasts is merely to observe that such a reaction is a natural response in the human male for which the evolutionary process has selected both for continuing the species and for bonding the man and woman together. This obsession can indeed degrade the woman, reducing her to an object, but it does not necessarily do so. To contend that a man who is fascinated by a woman's breasts (perhaps his wife's) is acting like a fourteen-year-old stealing a peek at *Playboy* is to remove his fascination from the context in which it occurs and to forget that, if there were not a bit of the fourteen-year-old in both the men and women of the species, humankind would soon cease to exist.

It would seem therefore that erotic desire, delicately and sensitively treated, would be not only proper for art with a Catholic inspiration but also indeed quite necessary to a healthy Christian worldview. Truth be told, this awareness has rarely surfaced in the history of Catholic art, nor is it current among those working in other traditions. Desire in the stories of John Updike, one of the greatest of contemporary American novelists, is an irresistible fate which draws men and women to their own destruction. There is much sexual coupling in his stories, but little sexual joy and virtually no happiness.

To leave erotic desire out of art that depicts human relationships is to distort the human condition beyond recognition. Consider the novels of Anthony Trollope, for example. His characters, men and women both, desperately want one another, but, caught in the taboos of his time, he could not attend to the nature of that want. His stories are not failures but devoid of a power they might otherwise have. They lack the irony and the tragedy, as well as the joy and satisfaction, which erotic desire introduces into the human condition. On the other hand, the theological novels of Susan Howatch, which revisit the Church of England a century after Trollope, are richer than Trollope's (in this respect) precisely because her men and women experience desire more explicitly and discuss it more directly.

The issue of erotic desire in art is especially pertinent to written art—fiction, poetry, drama. Classical forms of visual art may be erotic, but only rarely do they attempt to depict their subjects in the state of erotic desire. Thus, though the Zwinger gallery in Dresden abounds in nude figures, few of them could be considered erotic. But one artist among them, Carlo Cignani, in his depiction of Joseph and the wife of Potiphar, presents a jarring and thought-provoking image of erotic desire. Both participants are young, teenagers by today's standards. The half-naked girl is pretty, vulnerable, and very much in love. Her assault on Joseph seems almost innocent. He recoils in horror and turns to flee her. One understands Joseph's panic: if he yields to this attractive young woman, he will violate the law of his forefathers and risk both his life and hers. One also understands the surprise and humiliation of the young woman. In her culture her love for Joseph would be dangerous but hardly immoral.

Yet if one backs away from the title which the painter had to use to justify the story he tells, then one has an interesting depiction of man's attraction to the beauty of woman, his fear of it, and especially his fear of her as sexual aggressor. The painting could be easily construed as a parable of humankind's fear of an aggressively loving and demanding God.

This astonishing painting establishes that if one is to try to integrate erotic desire into art, one cannot present it only in its benign or virtuous manifestations.

In Boston's Museum of Fine Arts, a painting by Pieter Lastman portrays the wedding night of Tobias and his Sarah. The latter, partially undressed so as to reveal her lovely young breasts, sits on the edge of the bed watching anxiously as her new husband seems more interested in building a smelly fire than in making love to her. It is not unreasonable to assume that she loves this young man, perhaps the first of her husbands whom she loves, because he has treated her with respect. She is doubtless worried about whether the fiendish Asmodeus will take him away, too. Now she is also worried that he has turned away from her graciously offered body to build his fire out of fish innards. A nice boy, she might think, a very nice boy, but quite possibly out

Joseph and the Wife of Potiphar, by Carlo Cignani. Courtesy the Dresden National Art Museum.

The Wedding Night of Tobias and Sarah, by Pieter Lastman. Courtesy the Museum of Fine Arts, Boston.

of his mind. She cannot, of course, see Raphael wrapping chains around Asmodeus above their wedding bed.

The painting is charged with erotic tension. The only reason the artist can get away with its explicit sexuality is that the painting is based on a story in the Bible (or the Apocrypha, if you don't like the Catholic Bible). Both the Book of Tobit and the painting are stories which suggest that God takes care of young lovers, especially in those awkward and exciting moments when they enjoy one another's bodies for the first time as man and wife. God is especially present on the wedding night. It is but a step from that story to the idea that God is present in all passionate unions between married lovers, enjoys their love even more than they do. This is a profoundly Catholic idea, but one which is utterly unacceptable to many Catholics and which makes church leaders and teachers distinctly unhappy.

The notion that human arousal is a hint of divine arousal is most powerfully presented in some Renaissance paintings analyzed by the art critic Leo Steinberg (with the help of Jesuit John W. O'Malley).[3]

Steinberg observes that Renaissance art seems almost fixated on the genital organs of Jesus. Renaissance Madonnas often display to the onlooker Jesus' penis and testicles. Almost always Jesus is presented to the Magi stark naked. In Byzantine art the baby is always dressed in a proper, solemn, and imperial tunic. But, convinced as they were of the incarnation of Jesus, the artists of the *trecento* and the *quattrocento* seemed to have thought that it was absolutely essential that they manifest the full manhood of Jesus in their paintings. Father O'Malley confirms this interpretation in an analysis of sermons based on the best of the pre-Reformation Roman theologians—sermons sometimes preached in the presence of the popes.

Similarly, he sees the emphasis on the genital areas of Jesus' body in crucifixion and burial paintings as a depiction of the fortitude of the one who suffered. In this way, he suggests, the artists stressed that Jesus really died. Sexuality means mortality; a being without sex can only appear to die. Finally, Steinberg claims that some Renaissance artists depict the risen Jesus as sexually aroused, that indeed he comes out of the tomb in these paintings with an erect penis, covered by bulging loincloth. (The most notable example is the work of the Flemish painter Maerten van Heemskerck.) This is pretty strong stuff and would be offensive to more conservative Catholics and perhaps shocking to many moderate Catholics. It is, however, the way many Catholics of that era thought about the Incarnation, or the "humanization" of God in Jesus. Our style of reflecting on this mystery is no better inherently than was theirs, though their tastes may shock us.

Steinberg contends (and Father O'Malley agrees) that Renaissance Catholic humanism wished to insist on the full humanity of Jesus in opposition to the Arian and Monophysite heresies which in effect defined the divinity of Jesus in such a way that Jesus ended up not human at all. Curiously enough, and whatever may be the case today, during most of Christian history the humanity of Jesus was underestimated in theological attempts to balance the two realities bound together in Him. The Renaissance humanists did not intend to permit that.[4]

The Renaissance humanists did not easily get away with telling their daring artistic stories. During the Counter Reformation,

Catholic puritans painted loinclothes over Michelangelo's nudes,[5] chopped off penises and testicles (the striking Michelangelo of the risen Jesus has lost his penis, as though he shouldn't have had one in the first place), and denounced all nude art. The resulting distortions of great works are weird because they appeal to imaginations as sick as those of the iconoclasts who did the work of destruction.

At least the Catholic prudes didn't destroy the images as completely as did the Protestants of that era or the fanatical Byzantine iconoclasts of an earlier era.

Oddly enough, by no stretch of the imagination can any of the work of the Renaissance humanists be described as even mildly suggestive. The point then (and now) with the prudes is not that art was an "occasion of sin" but rather that it was disgusting. If human nature and human reproduction are disgusting—and a lot of Christians have thought so down through the ages—then one understands why they want to deny the humanity of Jesus: it too must be disgusting, unless it is stripped of its sexuality.

Neither Steinberg nor O'Malley dismiss this art as a reflection of folk practices of the time or of psychological disturbance. They are theological statements in artistic form, stories of God's love as revealed in the Incarnation.

It is thought to be bad taste even to raise questions about Jesus' sexuality. If one asks whether Jesus felt erotic attraction toward women, one is warned that the question is improper and perhaps blasphemous. Jesus is God, and how can God have erotic feelings? Yet Jesus is also human, and how can He be human and not have erotic feelings?

Leaving aside the point that in Jewish scriptures God often depicts Himself as inflamed with the love of His people, Jesus is also human and like humans in all things, sin alone excepted. If sexual desire as such is sinful, then Jesus would not feel sexual desire. But sexual desire is not in itself sinful, and one excludes it from the experiences of Jesus only by denying Him a full human nature. Therefore, it is extremely difficult to assert that Jesus did not find Himself drawn to women by their erotic appeal. Did Jesus, then, have erections? True, Jesus kept His sexual energies and feelings under control; He did not permit them to interfere with His mission; He never used, abused, or exploited women—quite the contrary, he treated them with more respect than any public figure of His age. But His restraint and respect were not that of an automaton indifferent to the erotic appeal of women. Did Jesus imagine sleeping with an attractive woman? Did He find certain kinds of womanly appeal more attractive than others? What healthy heterosexual male does not? Restraint does not mean repression.

I find in His relationship with the teenage women Mary and Martha (obviously very young because they were not yet married) a telling example of the restrained and disciplined affection a man can have for appealing young women who have a crush on him. I wonder if a man who had no sexual feelings could have been so sympathetic and so gentle with them. To those who tell me that these aspects of the story are peripheral to the intent of the scriptural author—and I have been told this in print—I reply that the Martha and Mary catena of stories (of which only two survive, alas) need not be based on literal events but does reveal the kind of man Jesus was.

The problem with Nikos Kazantzakis's novel and Martin Scorsese's film presentation of it is not that they present Jesus as a man with sexual feelings. Rather, they present married domesticity as a temptation when in fact it is a sacrament. There is no reason to believe that Jesus was married (despite the claims of fringe theologians), though nothing would change in His nature and mission if He were.

Nothing in the last two paragraphs is exceptionable. If these questions have had to wait for the late twentieth century to be answered, the reason is that the Christian heritage has been afraid to address them. However, merely to write such paragraphs is to ask for denunciations from Christian Fundamentalists, whether Catholic or Protestant. To go one step further and point out that some Catholic artists present Jesus as rising from the dead in a state of sexual arousal is to risk multiple denunciations dispatched to Rome.

I am not saying that Jesus was sexually aroused when He rose from the dead. I think the question is both irrelevant and pointless. I rather ask why some Catholic artists felt free to use such a metaphor and why, as far as we know, none of their contemporaries condemned them for it. What did their seemingly outrageous metaphor mean?

Steinberg and Father O'Malley argue that sexual arousal represents strength, fierce energy, passionate love. Surely strong arousal does fill a man with a sense of primal masculine power, concentrated energy, and passionate determination (it also stirs tenderness and affection, which are, alas, all too easily and all too often suppressed). This intense, dedicated dynamism in the works Steinberg studied is a metaphor for forces which filled the body of the risen Jesus.

It is only a metaphor. Indeed, the strength which surged through the body of Jesus who was dead and yet lived (as the story tells us) was doubtless even more powerful—and more loving. If modern people, confident of their own sexual liberation and sophistication, find the metaphor inappropriate, then they are free to dismiss it.

Erotic metaphors, as we have seen, are part of the Catholic religious sensibility, though Catholic teachers and leaders rarely address them. It is not likely that Bernini, St. John of the Cross, or Cignani have had much impact on Catholic laypeople through the ages. If the Catholic imagination were to have had any impact on the sexual behavior of Catholics, the influence would be more general: if grace is everywhere, it must be in sex, too.

It is virtually axiomatic that the negative sexual teachings of the Catholic Church interfere with the marital pleasures of Catholic husbands and wives. How could it be otherwise? Since the time of St. Augustine, the official Church has insisted that even between husband and wife sex was essentially for procreation. St. Augustine said that even marital sex directed toward procreation was at least a small sin because of the loss of self-control. Catholic spouses have been told that it is a grave sin to appear naked in one another's presence, and the Pontifical Commission on the Family warned in the 1970s that husbands and wives should beware of the risks of "unbridled lust" in their marriage relationship. Even the new "personalist" approach to married sex of the last two popes, so praised by some Catholic theologians, emphasizes restraint rather than passion, to say nothing of abandon. For generations, the heads of younger Catholics have been filled with a mixture of ignorance and superstition, fear and anxiety about sex. How could Catholics not have more sexual hang-ups than other Americans?

One might well be written off as a fool for questioning this alleged axiom. We read in fiction and nonfiction—we hear stories from both those who have left the Church in disgust and those who hang on inside its boundaries—of the terrible agony that Catholic sexual teaching has created for those who have been exposed to it. I do not question the authenticity or the pain of such experiences, but I remain to be convinced of their typicality—if only because I remain skeptical about how men and women could have lived married lives together during the last fifteen hundred years under the shadow of St. Augustine's negative view of human sexuality. Indeed, how many husbands and wives, or the parish clergy from whom they receive their religious teaching, have actually read St. Augustine, or papal encyclicals, or statements of the national hierarchies, or instructions of the Congregation for the Defense of the Faith?

So in my research I asked if there might have been another source by which Catholic insights on sex between husband and wife were passed down through the ages, a source which viewed passion between husband and wife with much more tolerance. To accomplish this task, I used a sociological model of two Catholic traditions—the high tradition and the popular tradition—and then fashioned some hypotheses which I could test against empirical data about the relative impact of the two traditions.

The high tradition is the Catholicism you learned in schools; the popular tradition is the Catholicism you learned in great part before you went to school. The former is contained in the teaching of theologians and the magisterium. It is cognitive, propositional, didactic. It is prosaic Catholicism. The latter is contained in the teaching of parents, family, neighbors, and friends. It is imaginative, experiential, narrative. It is poetic Catholicism.

All of the world religions have both kinds of traditions because all have their prose and poetic versions. Note, for example, in the Tanakh (the Jewish Bible) the prose history of the books of Kings and Samuel and the poetry of Isaiah and the Song of Songs. Of the four religions of the Book—Judaism, Protestantism, Catholicism, and Islam—Catholicism has the most richly developed popular tradition because it is least afraid of the imaginative dimension of religion. It is, to say the same thing in different words, the most sacramental of the four religions, the one most likely to see the transcendent lurking in the objects, events, and people of creation. It is the least likely to be afraid of contaminating God by using creation as a metaphor with which to describe Him.

As Catholic theologian John Shea has remarked to me, creation is grace, and the Church is a sacrament which bears witness to that truth.

If the high tradition is to be found in theology books and the documents of the councils, and the papacy, and various hierarchies of the world, the popular tradition is to be found in the rituals, the art, the music, the architecture, the devotions, the stories of ordinary people. If the former can be stated concisely at any given time in creeds which are collections of prose propositions, the latter is fluidly, amorphously, and illusively expressed in stories.

Prosaic people that we are, we members of the Catholic elite are inclined to believe that the real Catholicism is that of the high tradition. Doctrine and dogma are more important than experience and narrative. Literacy and education, we assume, will shortly dominate religion and all but the elderly will realize that the religion of image and story is but a step above superstition. The Christmas crib is popular Catholicism; the Decrees of Chalcedon are high Catholicism. The same story of God among us is told by both, the same fundamental reality of our faith is disclosed by both, the same rumor of angels is heard in both. Which, however, has more impact on the lives of ordinary Catholics? Anyone who thinks *homoiousios* is more important to ordinary folk than the Madonna and her Child is incurably prosaic—besides being wrong!

The popular tradition is more than just popular devotions. The Eucharist, for example, is more than just Corpus Christi processions (currently unfashionable) and visiting churches on Holy Thursday evening; it is, to risk translating poetry into prose, God among us at a family meal. In its essence, the popular tradition asserts—in the words of the country priest in Georges Bernanos's novel—that everything is grace.

Including sex.

In the words of the nuptial liturgy, "Love is our origin, love is our constant calling, love is our fulfillment in heaven. The love of man and woman is made holy in the sacrament of matrimony and becomes the mirror of your everlasting love."

It's very hard to think of that kind of love as sinful.

My distinction between the two traditions is merely a sociological model. Like all models it is a tentative description of reality into which much of what we know can be fit and which generates hypotheses for further testing. It is open to refinement and clarification as this testing occurs and even to being discarded and replaced as the process of clarification continues. One asks of such a model not whether it is true or false but whether it is useful in ordering the data and in producing testable hypotheses. I do not seek to impose it on you as the only way or the best way to examine religious reality. It is but one tool in a search for understanding.

Nor do I intend to suggest that the popular tradition is superior to the high tradition. Both are essential to any religious heritage. Because we are reflective beings, we must reflect on our religious experiences and narrative symbols and critique them with the powers of human reason. We must, as Paul Ricoeur says, make the pilgrimage from the first naïveté to the second naïveté. Catholicism, because of the very richness of its sacramentality, must always face the risk of slipping into superstition, folk religion, and paganism. The watchful criticism of the high tradition must always be in dialogue with the popular tradition when at its fringes such mistakes occur. On the other hand the high tradition, the tradition of prose and reflection, must listen carefully to the stories that the popular tradition tells or it will find itself cut off from the origins and the raw power of religion. The problem today, as I see it, is that there is very little dialogue between the two traditions and that indeed the high tradition, whether theological or magisterial, thinks it has a monopoly on Catholicism.

When the two traditions are in apparent conflict, I make no judgment about which ought to be followed. I predict that people will generally follow the popular tradition. I do not say that they *should* ignore what the theologians and the magisterium say but that, on average, it is likely that they will, because the popular tradition has so much more raw power and immediacy to their lives.

Note that I say "apparent conflict." There will always be tension between the two traditions, and that constant dialogue between them is essential. For example, when the present pope in his Apostolic Exhortation *Familiaris Consortio* said that the married laity, by virtue of the charism of the sacrament of matrimony, have a unique and indispensable contribution to make to the Church's understanding of sexual morality, this was surely dialogue between experience and prosaic theology. When there is apparent conflict between what the popular tradition experiences as crucial to the Catholic heritage and what the high tradition expresses cognitively as essential to the heritage, the conflict results from a breakdown of dialogue. That the reflecting Church and the experiencing Church, in such circumstances, are not listening to one another has about the same impact on the ecclesial organism as occurs to the human organism when the reflecting self and the experiencing self are not listening to one another.

Only in this century of universal education and literacy has the high tradition made a serious attempt to impose its Augustinian vision of the role of sexual love in marriage on the laity. Before that, the laity's attitudes toward married love, one may suspect, were shaped by the popular tradition, a (sometimes just barely) Christianized version of paganism—which included the rings, the crowns, and the gift of the bride by the father. Married love was good, it reflected God's love for us, husbands and wives should respect one another and treat each other as equals (more or less) and be grateful for the pleasures of sexual love. St. Augustine was heard in neither palace nor hovel and often not even by the clergy, who were poorly educated if not completely illiterate. The popular tradition flourished, reinforced by the sacramentality of Catholicism. So marriage beds were blessed to hallow the sexual love between bride and groom and no one thought it strange.

How does one find the popular tradition on marital sex? Since by definition it is not written down in books, it is usually not easy to find, even at the present time, though it is pervasive and its influence powerful. One must search the marriage rituals and blessings, the manuals for confessors, popular sermons on married love, love poetry and cemetery epitaphs, parish documents and registers, and passing allusions in such documents as *Parsifal*, *The Divine Comedy*, and *The Canterbury Tales*. Though most of the monographic research has yet to be done or even begun, even cursory consideration demonstrates that the popular tradition did not "buy" the Augustinian perspective. One need only compare the attitude toward sexual love of Wolfram von Eschenbach (the author of *Parsifal*) with that of St. Augustine to realize that the two men lived in different worlds.

How is the popular tradition transmitted? Through ritual and story, through song and dance, through priestly advice, through the instructions of one generation to another in the home and village (especially, on the subject of sex, through the advice of mothers to daughters), through the religious ambiance in which people lived. While these transmission mechanisms may seem weak and problematic, they are in fact, taken together, extraordinarily strong. If the popular tradition has dominated for most of Catholic history—and I argue that it has—the reason is that it has been reinforced by the enchanted imagination of Catholicism, which senses intuitively that the body of the beloved is grace.

The essence of this tradition's take on married love, to use modern terminology, is that sexual pleasure heals the frictions and conflicts of the common life and reinforces the bond between husband and wife. Not to understand this truth, married men and women down through the ages would have argued, is not to understand anything at all about marriage. Then and now, their parish clergy have tended to agree with them—and the "now" part of that assertion can be proved with empirical data, as a recent *Los Angeles Times* study of the priesthood shows.

Is it not possible that the Augustinian theory of marital sex has no impact on Catholic behavior? Is it possible that, to go one step further, the popular tradition might have a positive impact on Catholic sexual behavior? If so, then it is appropriate to examine the hypothesis that Catholic sexual behavior in marriage is no more inhibited by the high tradition than is the sexual love of anyone else and in fact may be reinforced by the sacramentality of the popular tradition. Catholic sexual hang-ups, in other words, may be no worse than anyone else's.

I have six indicators from two representative samples of American married people (one with 1,325 cases and the other with 4,414 cases) against which to test these expectations:

1. Frequency of sexual intercourse.
2. Persistence of sexual intercourse as one grows older.
3. Sexual playfulness (a scale combining such matters as prolonged periods of sexual play between spouses, mutual undressing, showers or baths together, swimming in the nude with one's spouse, making love outdoors, purchase of erotic undergarments, and experimentation with various sexual techniques).
4. A stronger Catholic effect in marriages where both partners are Catholic.
5. The strength of the correlation between frequency of intercourse and psychological well-being and personal happiness (an indirect measure of the "enjoyment" of sexual intercourse).
6. The strength of the correlation between frequent sex and marital satisfaction as measured by the response that one would

marry the same spouse again if one had a chance to do it again (a second indirect measure of the "delight" in the spouse).

In the logic of my argument three outcomes are possible.

First, if Catholic scores are lower than those of others, the Catholic high tradition has inhibited Catholic sexual activity, and Catholics have more sexual hang-ups on the average than others.

Second, if Catholic sexual behavior on these six indicators is no different from that of other Americans, it would follow that the high tradition has at least not inhibited married sex among Catholics. Catholics have no more sexual hang-ups than anyone else, perhaps because the high tradition no longer has any effect on their behavior, if it ever did.

Third, if Catholic scores are on the average higher than those of others, then Catholics must have fewer sexual hang-ups than others and enjoy sex more, especially if they are married to another Catholic, and even more so if—to add a seventh indicator—they have a "spousal" image of God.

My findings are as follows:

1. Sixty-eight percent of Catholics, as opposed to 56 percent of others, engage in sexual union at least once a week. This finding is confirmed by the fact that it is also reported by spouses of Catholics who are not themselves Catholics.

2. Frequency of intercourse declines with age less precipitously among Catholics than among others, so that Catholics are one quarter again more likely than others to have sex at least once a week when they are fifty-five or more years old (50 percent versus 40 percent).

3. Catholics score significantly higher on the sexual playfulness scale. For example, Catholics are half again as likely (30 percent versus 20 percent) to say they have purchased erotic undergarments either often or sometimes—a flimsy sacramentality (to indulge in a pun), but a sacramentality nonetheless. (If such garments are useful in arraying the spouse as an alluring person, they surely are small hints of God's allure—at least to those who see the whole of creation as a metaphor for God.)

4. On all three of these measures the effect is strongest in endogamous Catholic marriages.

5. The correlation between frequency of intercourse and personal well-being is .12 for Catholics and .06 for others; marital happiness correlates with sexual frequency at .18 for Catholics and .12 for others. Catholics "enjoy" sex more. Catholics who have sex infrequently are lower in personal happiness than others and Catholic who have sex frequently are higher than others on personal happiness. Moreover, this special Catholic correlation is observed *only* among those Catholics who imagine God as a spouse.

6. The correlation between frequency of intercourse and the response that one would marry the same spouse again is .32 for Catholics and .15 for others. Catholics who have sex infrequently are lower in this "delight in the spouse" than are others, and Catholics who have sex frequently are higher in this delight than others. The delight is even stronger among Catholic women than among Catholic men.

7. Furthermore, the sexual playfulness scale (which exists in only one of the two studies) accounts completely for the higher intercourse rate of Catholics. In sociological terms, in a regression equation the playfulness scale reduces the difference in in-

tercourse rates to statistical insignificance. Catholics engage in intercourse more frequently, it would seem, *because* they approach sex more playfully. Moreover, Catholic rates of sexual playfulness are especially high if they have gracious images of God, that is, if they see benign human relationships (mother, spouse, friend, lover) as metaphors of God.

8. Finally, in the other study, the image of God as spouse rather than master accounts completely for the difference between Catholics and other Americans in frequency of sex. Catholics have higher rates of sexual love because of the impact on them of the story of human passion as a hint of divine passion.

The model of the two traditions predicts that Catholics have sex more often, they are more playful in their sexual encounters, and they enjoy sex more. Of our three possible outcomes, the third set of predictions turns out to be accurate.

These findings, which substantially strengthen the theory of a distinctively enchanted Catholic imagination, will offend two groups of people—those who desperately want to believe that most Catholics are suffering terribly because of the Church's sexual teaching and that therefore the Church is coming apart; and those Church leaders who still see married sex through the eyes of St. Augustine and want to warn the laypeople of the dangers of unbridled lust. As if, in the words of a layman to me, the real problem in most marriages is not too much *bridled* lust. Neither response comprehends the durability, the pervasiveness, the influence, or the appeal of the popular tradition as it passes on from generation to generation the sacramental imagination, that poetry of Catholicism which keeps most Catholics in the Church.

I am not arguing that St. Augustine's fears about loss of self-control are invalid. One need merely read the stories in the daily papers or watch the evening news to understand that humans do terrible harm to other humans because of the sexual drive. Sex is potentially both demonic and tragic; indeed, both the demonic and the tragic aspects of sexuality affect the personality of each of us. The popular tradition arguably underestimates the dangers, but it has surely protected the Catholic laity from living married lives in St. Augustine's somber shadow.

In an enchanted world, the beloved is both enchanting and frustrating. In happy relations, enchantment outweighs frustration. Catholics have an advantage in that deep down in their imaginations there is a sense, perhaps never explicitly stated or even realized, that the lover and the beloved are supposed to be grace for one another. This instinct, which links Bernini and St. John of the Cross and the Sarum ritual and Van Heemskerck and the nuptial Eucharist to the contemporary Catholic spouse placing an order from the Victoria's Secret catalogue or enticing the beloved into the shower, could exist only in an enchanted world.

The Mother Love of God

I heard the story in third grade and have never forgotten it. I tell it at homily times often, especially on feasts of the mother of Jesus. I understand it much better today than I did in the past, though that increase of understanding does not add anything to my appreciation of it, which is surely pre-philosophical, pre-theological, and pre-sociological.

One day Himself was going on a tour of the heavenly city, much like the monsignor tours his parish or the mayor his city. Heaven is, after all, the city that works. Everything seemed in order. The hedges were properly trimmed, the lawns properly cut, all the gold and ivory polished and glowing. The choirs were practicing at the scheduled times and had never sounded better.

But then, as He walked down the main street, He noticed that there were some people wandering around as bold as brass who had no business being there at all, at all. Some of them should

OPPOSITE: *Madonna and Child*, by Bottega di Tomaso di Vigilia. Photo by Leonard de Selva, courtesy CORBIS.

not have been admitted without a long period of service in pur-
gatory. Others would make it only on the day before the Last
Judgment, and a few of them only on very special appeal to the
Holy Spirit.

So He goes out to the gates of the city and there is your man
at his workstation with his Dell computer, and his tiara (for
Peter, you know, was the first pope, even if he didn't realize it),
and his fishing rod.

"Well, Simon Peter, you've let me down again, and yourself
with the keys of heaven."

"What have I done this time?" your man says with a loud sigh.

"Haven't you let in a lot of folks who have no business being
here at all, at all?"

"I have not," says the first pope.

"Well then who has?"

"You don't want to know."

"Yes, I do."

"Well," says Simon Peter with a very loud sigh, "didn't I tell
them that there's no way they can come in and then don't I slam
the gate on them?"

"And then what?"

"Then don't they go around to the back door and doesn't your
mother let them in!"

Taken with theological literalness, the story is absurd. But on
the level of narrative symbol, it summarizes the function of the
Mary metaphor in the Catholic imagination: she represents the
Mother Love of God, the generous and loving, life-giving power
of God, the tenderness of God, the fertility of God, the nurturing of God.[1]

The image of Mary the mother of Jesus distinguishes the Catholic religious sensibility from all others. She pushes the envelope of the Catholic imagination as far as it can be pushed by hinting that there is a maternal dimension in God as well as a paternal one and thus absorbs and purifies and transforms all the female deities who came before (Nut, Astarte, Venus, Brigid).

Do I mean that Mary is a goddess, like the other goddesses?

The answer is no and yes. Mary was a human person, not a divine person. Catholics do not worship Mary, as much as the Protestant heritage at its most ungenerous has claimed they do. Rather, through Mary Catholics worship the Mother Love of God. However, in the Catholic heritage her image has a similar, though not identical, function to that of the womanly deities of the nature religions: she discloses that the Power Which Is Responsible has a tender, gentle, life-giving, nurturing dimension. In other words, God loves like a mommy as well as like a daddy.[2]

This is social science analysis of a metaphor, which of course diminishes the symbol by reducing poetry to prose. I am not suggesting that Catholics, unsophisticated in the past and sometimes only marginally more sophisticated in the present, have explicitly interpreted the metaphor that way. One doesn't have to interpret poetry unless one is a literary critic. One doesn't have to take apart a metaphor unless one is a scholar. Rather, I am arguing that, in the art and the music and the poetry of those Catholics, Mary's image clearly reflects the tenderness of God.

Do we need an image of a woman to reflect the tenderness of God? In the absolute sense we do not. But the human experience of gender differentiation being what it is, it helps to have such an image, and it is probably inevitable that one will develop.

It is not the doctrines about her, nor the theologies which have developed around those doctrines, which constitute the image's appeal. I do not intend to reject or criticize these doctrines and theologies: they are the superstructure built on the infrastructure of the stories. Long before the doctrines were elaborated and before the theologies were written, the stories were told. It is the story that God loves us like a mother as well as a father—rarely expressed in such explicit language—that is at the core of the appeal of the Mary metaphor.

Gerard Manley Hopkins, the haunted nineteenth-century Jesuit poet, pointed at the essence of the Catholic sensibility about the mother of Jesus when he tied together the fertility of spring, the fertility of Mary, and the fertility of God. Indeed, his "May Magnificat" is as perfect an example of the analogical imagination fervently at work as one might want:

May is Mary's month, and I
Muse at that and wonder why:
    Her feasts follow reason,
    Dated due to season—

Candlemas, Lady Day;
But the Lady Month, May,
    Why fasten that upon her,
    With a feasting in her honor?

Is it only its being brighter
Than the most are must delight her
    Is it opportunest
    And flowers finds soonest

Ask of her, the mighty mother
Her reply puts this other

Question: What is Spring
Growth in every thing—

Flesh and fleece, fur and feather,
Grass and greenworld all together;
   Star-eyed strawberry-breasted
   Throstle above her nested

Cluster of bugle blue eggs thin
Forms and warms the life within;
   And bird and blossom swell
   In sod or sheath or shell.

All things rising, all things sizing
Mary sees, sympathising
   With that world of good,
   Nature's motherhood.

Their magnifying of each its kind
With delight calls to mind
   How she did in her stored
   Magnify the Lord.

Well but there was more than this:
Spring's universal bliss
   Much, how much to say
   To offering Mary May.

When drops-of-blood-and-foam-dapple
Bloom lights the orchard-apple
   And thicket and thorp are merry
   With silver-surfed cherry

And azuring-over greybell makes
Wood banks and brakes wash wet like lakes
   And magic cockoo call
   Caps, clear, and clinches all—

This ecstasy all through mothering earth
Tells Mary her mirth till Christ's birth
  To remember and exultation
  In God who was her salvation.

When it links the fertility of nature and the fertility of a woman with the fertility of God, the Catholic imagination risks being profoundly offensive. In effect it seems to be regressing to the fertility cults which tempted ancient Israel. The Holy One made it clear to His people that He controlled all fertility but totally transcended it. The forces of fertility were not to be worshiped because they were His servants. How could Catholicism have turned its back on that lesson and introduced Mary, a mere human woman, as an intermediary between God, the giver of all life, and humankind?

The question is a legitimate one. However, it makes God's giving and nurturing of life and creation's giving and nurturing of life seem completely discontinuous. It denies not only any participation of the latter in the former but even the use of the latter as a metaphor, a hint, however imperfect, of the former. The Catholic imagination, bravely or foolishly, depending on your perspective, swept aside such fears and first permitted the Mary cult to develop and then encouraged it.

As late as the twelfth century, the Vatican was uneasy about the Normans' propensity to dedicate their soaring cathedrals to "Our Lady." But the popular tradition, was not to be denied. Only a generation or two away from paganism, the Normans were building shrines to the Christian "goddess" of spring. They were God's churches of course, but hers too, and that was that. Given the decisions already made about absorbing and "baptizing" everything that was good, true, and beautiful in paganism, the development was probably inevitable.

My colleague and friend Sidney Verba and I were walking on the Left Bank on an Easter Sunday afternoon just after Le General had cleaned Notre Dame de Paris. It was during the Vietnam War. Sidney, in Paris on a sabbatical, paused and looked up at the great church.

"It hasn't been a good year," he said, "not with all the terrible things that are happening. Yet whenever I feel discouraged I come over here and look at that and say to myself, a species which has built something like Notre Dame may deserve to survive."

The sudden, dramatic appearance of the Norman cathedrals in France in the twelfth century is an astonishing phenomenon, though we tend to take it for granted. Descendants of Norse pirates, only a generation or two at the most distant from paganism, the churchmen, nobility, craftsmen, and artists who created these wondrous spaces might have been weak in their theology and still superstitious. Like their Celtic predecessors, they may have danced by the sides of lakes, but they knew who Our Lady was, and in an interlude of almost dizzy creativity they celebrated her as a spring goddess with spring temples. What did the Mary metaphor mean in the late Middle Ages? Go to Paris or Chartres or Amiens and learn what it meant: life and superabundant life. We have not seen anything like it, not really, ever since.

Of the actual mother of Jesus we know almost nothing historically. What we do know does not really account for the power of the metaphor she has become. Four New Testament scenes, however, have been seized on by the Catholic imagination—the visit by Gabriel, the birth in the cave in Bethlehem, the Babe in her arms (the classic Madonna pose), and the Pieta, which depicts her receiving the dead body of her Son. If such images were attractive to great artists (the Botticelli of his *Annunciation*, the Raphael of his Madonnas, the Michelangelo of his *Pieta*, or the anonymous carver of a medieval ivory Madonna), the reason was that the stories and the lurking metaphors had enormous appeal to the human imagination. Once humankind recognized the Mary stories, they became irresistible. That's the way God loves us, the stories say (to submit them once more to analysis), the way a mother loves her baby!

As important as the Christmas crib scene (perhaps invented in the High Middle Ages by St. Francis of Assisi) is, the central Mary story is the Madonna image, one that is preceded by depictions of mother goddesses and their sons, though quite different from Mary and Jesus. Like all mother-and-child religious imagery, this central story is based ultimately on the image of a mother with a baby in her arms, an image irresistible to human nature since it represents the ongoing triumph of fertility over morbidity, of life over death. In the Byzantine churches, the icons of the God-Bearer are rich and stylized. In the West, as the High Middle Ages turned into the Renaissance, the Madonnas which filled the museums of Europe became less mystical and more human and earthy—placid and attractive peasant girls with fat and happy babies (though occasionally one encounters a bumptious baby, or one who, like Cupid with Venus, touches his mother's chin).

At times these Madonnas—those painted by Raphael for example—have been accused of being too human, devoid of spirituality. In the spirit of Raphael's era, however, this effect was his purpose. The real Mary and the real Jesus surely did not look

A detail of Michelangelo's *Pieta*. Photo by David Lees, courtesy
CORBIS.

particularly spiritual or mystical. Together they were a peasant mother and a peasant child, both doubtless appealing but hardly seeming to be engaged in ecstatic experiences.

> *Ave maris stella*
> *Dei mater alma*
> *Atque semper virgo*
> *Felix coeli porta.*

It seems to Catholics that to turn away from the stories in stone and paint and song with haughty disdain is to miss the point completely and perhaps just a little perversely.

If one says, "but we do not know what the actual Mary was like," then the response is, if a prose response is required, "but we do know what her Son was like, so we can guess what kind of a woman she must have been."

The great sinner (by his own admission) Francois Villon once decided to sing a hymn to Mary:

> Lady of Heaven and earth, and therewithal
> Crowned Empress of the nether clefts of Hell,
> I, thy poor Christian, on thy name do call
> Commending me to thee, with thee to dwell,
> Albeit in nought I be commendable.
> But all mine undeserving may not mar
> Such mercies as thy sovereign mercies are;
> Without the which (as true words testify)
> No soul can reach thy Heaven so fair and far.
> Even in this faith I choose to live and die.
> O excellent Virgin Princess! Thou didst bear
> King Jesus, the most excellent comforter,
> Who even of this our weakness craved a share

And for our sake stooped to us from on high,
Offering to death His young life sweet and fair.
Such as He is, Our Lord, I Him declare,
And in this faith I choose to live and die.

Centuries later T. S. Eliot thought there was a power still left in the Mary metaphor. In his passionate cry for salvation at the end of "Ash Wednesday," he begs

Blessed sister, holy mother, spirit of the fountain, spirit of the
   garden,
Suffer us not to mock ourselves with falsehood
Teach us to care and not to care
Teach us to sit still
Even among these rocks, Our peace in His will
And even among these rocks Sister, mother
And spirit of the river, spirit of the sea,
Suffer me not to be separated

And let my cry come unto Thee.

The Mary image, then, has proven irresistible to poets and artists of many different faiths through the ages—and to some, like Henry Adams, who had very little faith. One wonders how such a glorious image could possibly offend. Nonetheless, there is solid instinct in the Reformation's resistance to superstition. Metaphors can easily be abused. There was and is still abuse of the Mary metaphor. But one need not throw out the baby's mother with the bathwater.

Harder to understand is the distaste of many contemporary Catholic clergy and intellectuals for the Mary metaphor. Admittedly, some strange and offputting movements and devotions have claimed her for their own. She has become a negative sex image, a patron of right-wing causes, a focus of dubious devotions. Metaphors can be abused, misused, used inappropriately. But that does not destroy the power of the metaphor. How could anyone give up on an image as dominant as the Madonna image has been for at least a millennium and a half? Yet, in fact, the Mary metaphor seems to be in trouble. In recent years, there have been only a few lyric poems, practically no distinguished paintings, and only monstrous churches (of which the most monstrous of all is the great concrete dump built on a peat bog at the town of Knock in Ireland). The document on Mary was jettisoned at the Second Vatican Council. Professional Catholic ecumenists are uneasy about the metaphor. Catholic feminists announce that she simply won't do. Pope John Paul II's devotion to Mary seems to many to strike a false note. Has not the Mary image faded from the consciousness of ordinary Catholics? Can one really expect to find a correlation between the Mary metaphor and Catholic attitudes and behavior at the end of the twentieth century?

In John Powers's play, "Do Black Patent Leather Shoes Really Reflect Up?" there is a scene in which the second grade, performing its annual Mary crowning, begins to sing "Flowers of the Rarest." The night we were there, the audience joined in the chorus: "O Mary, we crown thee with blossoms today." I asked Mr. Powers if this was an unusual event. "They do it every night," he replied. "If they stop singing it, I'll begin to worry."

William McCready made the same point a number of years ago. "All the Catholic Church has left is the Blessed Mother and the Catholic schools. Neither has been very popular since the Second Vatican Council. Yet both have managed to survive. Indeed, Mary, probably the most important culture symbol in two thousand years of Western history, is alive and well in North America, even among young people."

In a study of Catholic young adults, the Mary image proved to be stronger than either the Jesus image or the God image. As Professor Terry Sullivan, a member of the study staff remarked, "Bernard of Clairvaux was right: If you fear the father, go to the son. If you fear the son, go to the mother."[3]

More than 75 percent of the young adults said they were "extremely likely" to think of Mary as "warm," "patient," "comforting," or "gentle." Sixty-five percent of the respondents checked all four words as "extremely likely," while only 50 percent rated Jesus as high on all four items. Moreover, our Madonna Scale (one point for each of the four words checked as "extremely likely") correlated positively with social commitment, frequency of prayer, concern for racial justice, and sexual fulfillment in marriage. Mary is not only still fashionable but also, it seems, still "relevant."

How can this be? Have not the Catholic schools deemphasized Mary? Has not the Church played down doctrine in a quest for ecumenical understanding?

I was not surprised by the persistence of Mary, although I was astonished by the vigor of her persistence. We had theoretical reasons for expecting such a persistence. Womanly cosmic personages in whom divine tenderness is embodied are irresistible. Stories which suggest that God loves us as a mother loves her child, indeed that at the very core of the cosmos (or cosmoi, if one accepts certain modern theories of theoretical cosmology) is Mother Love, never lose their appeal. Hence the near universality of mother symbols in religions.

Most of us have had the experience of having a mother (or a mother surrogate). Similarly, most of us at one time or another have the experience of either being potentially a mother or being able to join with a potential mother in an activity that enables her to become a mother. Conceding to the psychoanalysts and feminists all the ambivalence that one experiences in relationship to one's mother, the appeal of a warm, gentle, patient, comforting mother is still powerful in our species. Consider the annual impact of the Nativity scene or the attractiveness of a young mother holding a baby in her arms in an airport boarding lounge.

The motherhood experience is one of the most powerful sacraments in our lives. It can be an overwhelming experience of grace, representing the persistence of life and, indeed, of life treated with tenderness and care. A religious symbol that resonates with and replicates the grace experience of maternity will have perennial appeal. Hence the presence of womanly deities (or cosmic personages, if you will) in almost all of the world's religions.

Each human being must decide whether there is a plan in the universe and a purpose in his or her life. Often these matters are inconclusive. Yet often, too, it appears that there is graciousness at work. The stories of God that resonate with the appearance of grace cannot be eradicated from human consciousness. If Whoever-is-behind-it-all is kind and good, and sometimes it appears that He might not be, then there is reason to hope. If, additionally, the Whoever-is-behind-it-all loves us with the tenderness and warmth of a mother toward her newborn babe, there is reason to celebrate Her love. Maternity may or may not be an accurate story of God, but the attractiveness of the possibility makes the "mother story" virtually irresistible and guarantees the survival of the story, no matter how much the elite may think it outmoded.

Mary survives among young adults for the same reason that she has been an appealing sacrament for fifteen hundred years. She is too good a story of God to pass up. Whether the story she represents is too good to be true is another matter, though on this subject the Catholic sensibility traditionally has been confident.

With all this in mind, I formulated a number of hypotheses:

1. The Madonna Scale would correlate with positive experiences with motherhood as a child.

2. The scale would also correlate with positive experiences with a spouse, particularly in the most intimate acts of the relationship—"sexual fulfillment," as our questionnaire called it—because motherhood and spousal intimacy share an openness to the human body.

3. Positive experiences of motherhood as a child would further correlate with sexual fulfillment in marriage and be channeled, at least in part, through the Madonna image.

4. The Madonna image would correlate at a much higher level with personal prayer than would doctrinal orthodoxy.

Our maternity measure was composed of four items: a description of the mother's approach to religion as "joyous"; frequent taking of Holy Communion on the part of the mother; the mother involvement, as at least an equal to the father, in family decision making; and the mother's strong religious effect on the respondent. Sexual fulfillment was one of a list of dimensions of marital satisfaction ranked from "excellent" to "poor." The doctrinal orthodoxy scale was composed of such matters as papal infallibility, papal primacy, mortally sinful obligation to attend Mass each week, and the existence of the devil and hell.

The first four hypotheses were all true at statistically significant levels for both men and women in the United States and Canada. Women have higher scores on the Madonna Scale than men, but there are no important differences in the correlations with gender regarding any of the other findings.

For Catholics, a positive experience with your mother while growing up leads to a positive experience with your spouse. Your image of Mary is the conduit linking these two experiences. Mary connects the story of your childhood to the story of your marriage. Small wonder she's important.

There is no statistically significant relationship between doctrinal orthodoxy and prayer—in fact, the relation is 0.07 in the opposite direction. But the Madonna Scale correlates with frequency of prayer. Images, not doctrinal propositions, lead people to prayer.

Neither the Jesus Scale nor the God Scale correlates with experiences in either family of origin or family of procreation. Mary is the story of God that links the two aspects of your story.

When husband and wife alike are high on the Madonna Scale, it is half again as likely that they will both say that their sexual fulfillment is "excellent." (Questionnaires were filled out independently—not that anyone would be likely to conspire about their image of Mary.) Furthermore, among those families where both husband and wife are high on the Madonna Scale, the correlation between one spouse's description of the quality of the sexual relationship and the other's description of it becomes higher as the years together increase. As couples, if we share a common story of God in the Mary image, we come to share more and more a common story of our own sexual relationship.

Some feminist critics of devotion to Mary, most notably Marina Warner in her *Alone of All Her Sex*, have argued that the Mary symbolism traditionally was used to support a "conservative" approach to the role of women, emphasizing fulfillment in the home and family to the exclusion of all else and placing too high a value on passivity and fertility. They have also contended that this tradition has "spoiled" the image for contemporary women. I am in no position to discuss the historical impact of Marian imagery on women in years past. I will also concede to writers like Warner the possibility that the image has been spoiled for them. However, I can assure them that the Mary image does not play any such conservative role for today's young men or women.

There is no difference between those who are high on the Madonna Scale and those who are low on the scale in attitudes toward birth control, divorce, or abortion of pregnancies likely to result in handicapped children. High and low scorers marry at about the same age, have about the same number of children, and make the same estimates of future family size (low, but higher than the estimates of those who are not Catholics). Nor does a strong Marian image impede college graduation, work after marriage, economic success, or a propensity to reject the idea that a working mother harms her children. Those who are high on the Madonna Scale, however, are more likely to reject abortion on demand and to disapprove of living together before marriage.

I presume that young people learn about Mary from their mothers. From whom else would they? I also speculate that they learn about her *very early* in life as they are told the Christmas story. The woman by the crib, they are told, is God's "mommy," a proposition with which children have no difficulty. We all have a mommy, don't we? From such an insight it is but a small jump to say that God loves like a mommy. The story is born again.

Rather surprisingly, Mary's image is almost as strong with spouses of Catholics who are not themselves Catholic as it is with Catholics. Sixty-two percent say they are "extremely likely" to think of her as "warm," 67 percent as "gentle," 52 percent as "patient," and 56 percent as "comforting." Forty percent of the spouses who are not Catholics endorse as "extremely likely" all four items on the Madonna Scale—not quite as many as Catholic spouses, of whom 65 percent do so, but still the percentage is astonishingly high. There is also a correlation, even among spouses who are not Catholic, between a high Madonna score and frequent prayer: 52 percent of the spouses high on the Madonna Scale pray almost every day, as opposed to 40 percent of those who are low. (More than half of the Methodists and Baptists endorse all four Madonna items, as do 37 percent of those spouses who report no religious affiliation.) Mary may actually be an asset to ecumenical discourse instead of a liability.

If Mary images are so important to Catholics, ought not Catholics be more likely to support equal rights and opportunities for women than do other Americans? On the average, they do.

The question is simple enough and an answer not hard to obtain. Since 1972, NORC has been asking in its (usually) annual General Social Survey a battery of questions about women:

[Should] women . . . take care of their homes and leave the running of the country to men[?]

Do you approve or disapprove of a married woman in business or industry if she has a husband capable of supporting her?

If your party nominated a woman for president, would you vote for her if she were qualified for the job?

The three items, not surprisingly, fit into a scale on which Catholics had a higher score than Protestants, even when Southern Baptists were separated from other Protestants. (Jewish women had the highest scores of all; Jewish men and Irish Catholic men and women tied for second place; liberal Protestants had higher scores than the Catholic average.) These differences were not reduced by controls for educational achievement and region of the country, but they were reduced to statistical insignificance when a control for the religious imagination (via the Grace Scale) was introduced. Once again, the interaction between Catholic background, religious imagery (God as mother, spouse, friend, and lover), and feminism was important. Catholics with low scores on the Grace Scale were less likely to be "pro woman" than their Protestant counterparts, but there was no correlation between grace and feminism for Protestants and a strong correlation for Catholics: the Protestant line was flat and the Catholic line went up sharply. The greatest difference between Catholics and Protestants was at the high end of the Grace Scale.

The leadership of the Church is still of mixed mind about the equality of women. In theory, it now celebrates their equality, but in practice it refuses to share top-level power with women. Moreover, it excludes women from priestly ordination, often with the thoroughly tasteless remark that a woman's body is not a suitable vessel for the sacrament of Holy Orders. Yet almost two-thirds of American Catholics support the ordination of women (men more likely than women, priests more likely than laypeople).

The sacramental imagination, when working properly, apparently does sense a correlation between a lurking God and equality of women. It does perceive, however dimly, that a woman's body is as much a sacrament of God's love as a man's body.

Even in an era with no great churches or paintings or music, in which the sacramentality of erotic love is scarcely defended and little attention paid to Mary, the sacramental imagination, passed on implicitly by popular tradition, clearly has enormous residual power.

Community

I talian American films, from *Mean Streets* through *Moonstruck*, *Sleepers*, and *Johnny Brasco*, display consistency in their settings and characters. There is almost always an uncle who is "connected," a priest, a tough kid, a rebellious young woman, a suspicious working-class father, a crooked cop, an outspoken mother or grandmother. Robert DeNiro is often present. Baptisms, marriages, and funerals are celebrated with elaborate expense, if not a lot of taste. One can hardly avoid the obligatory scenes in a parish church, a grocery store, a tavern with a bar and pool tables and an always running television set, an "athletic" club in which a "wise guy" sits with his back against the wall as if waiting for the coming of the inevitable hit men, a ball game in Shea Stadium. And all the characters wave their hands when they talk, ya know what I mean?

Some of this characterization may be stereotypical. Most Italian Americans are not connected, though they may know someone

OPPOSITE: A scene from Nancy Savoca's *Household Saints*. Left to right: Michael Rispoli, Vincent D'Onofrio, Victor Argo, Joe Grifasi.

who is—but what urban American does not? Italian Americans are more likely to be both white collar and professional workers than the national average. Some of them engage in quiet family dinners with almost no shouting. Some may even talk without waving their hands, though I haven't met any such, and for all I know waving your hands and shouting when you talk is the most natural style of human communication. Certainly, stereotypes and false rumors like those said to have interfered with a Mario Cuomo presidential run are intolerable.

Nonetheless, most Italian American films are about an intense family life, intricate extended family relations, and a close-knit neighborhood community.[1] The neighborhood is not just a setting: it is a reality that impinges on the whole story. A character in Thomas Kelly's novel *Payoff*, about Irish gangs in the Hell's Kitchen neighborhood of New York during the 1980s, remarks that he will not accept as his boss "some fat Italian who's not neighborhood." The ethnicity and the fat are not important—it's the last word that counts.

Lee Lourdeaux, in his brilliant book *Italian and Irish Filmmakers in America*,[2] insists plausibly that *Apocalypse Now* is really less about Joseph Conrad's *Heart of Darkness* than about an Italian American family conflict and that Frank Capra's *It's a Wonderful Life* is really the story of an Italian village in an American disguise. He might just as well have said that it was about an Italian American neighborhood transferred upstate. What an even more wonderful film it would have made if it were set in a neighborhood in Queens with the usual Italian American cast!

Clearly, family and local community are overwhelming issues among Italian American filmmakers. They do not choose to make such films simply because they find the settings interesting or because they have discovered that audiences like the trappings of Italian American culture, though these motives are doubtless at work, too. They choose their settings because in a certain sense that's all they know. They do not use the Catholic sacramental rituals merely to provide local color but because, whatever their relationship to the Church and its sacramental system, the rituals are an important part of their lives, a forceful way of presenting their experiences of critical turning points.

The works of Martin Scorsese are the quintessential illustrations of the use of the Catholic sense of community and Catholic symbols in American filmmaking. Scorsese could not have made his autobiographical films and especially not *Mean Streets* without using these images. It was not a matter of choice but of necessity. Incidentally, the best recreation of the street scenes in Italian American neighborhoods is that of Nancy Savoca in the film *Household Saints*, which I discussed earlier. This recreation is so well done, in fact, that you don't even notice it. Scorsese is good but Savoca is better, perhaps because no mere male can possibly have a feel for the concrete details of a setting that a woman has.

Charlie, the protagonist of *Mean Streets*—played by a very young Harvey Keitel, young but still cool—is a deeply conflicted man, caught up in his Uncle Johnny's corruption, swayed by strong sexual desire (focused on Teresa [Amy Robinson] whom Uncle Johnny calls sick in the head because she has epilepsy) and yet deeply desiring to be a good and even holy Catholic, a modern St. Francis of Assisi. Lourdeaux is wrong, I believe, to say that the desire for holiness is absorbed from Irish clergy. Charlie is an authentically devout Italian male. Rarely do Irish youths go around hoping to be St. Francis. (After I met Mario Cuomo I

Robert DeNiro (left) and Harvey Keitel in Martin Scorsese's *Mean Streets*.

came to see him as the same kind of devout Italian male, though not as conflicted as poor Charlie.) The theme that sorrow for one's sins is worked out not in church but in the streets runs through the film—most reviewers missed it, although the theme is stated at the very beginning. The quest for holiness occurs, and forgiveness is earned, on the mean streets themselves. Or so says the film. Forgiveness is a gift that cannot be earned. If he were more sophisticated theologically, Charlie would say that what is worked out on the streets is love responding to Love.

The quest for goodness for Charlie means protecting the delicious and outspoken Teresa and especially her cousin, the half-mad and perhaps brain-damaged Johnny Boy (an almost unrecognizably young Robert DeNiro). Uncle Johnny warns against both people: Charlie ought not to risk his chances for prosperity. If he is careful, he will own his own restaurant, one that presently belongs to a man who cannot meet his debt payments on Uncle Johnny's loan. (The man will stay on, it appears, as manager.) But Charlie cannot abandon either Teresa or Johnny Boy. They are both "neighborhood"; they are both "connected" to his family. They are part of his world. If you exploit or abandon your own people, who are you? What do you have left? What point is there in life? He tells his friend Michael—the sleek loan shark to whom Johnny Boy is deeply in hock—that you just don't charge loan-shark rates to someone from the "neighborhood." But Johnny Boy ignores Charlie's warnings and, seemingly bent on self-destruction, keeps missing payments to Michael. Finally, Michael drives by a car in which Johnny Boy, Teresa, and Charlie are riding and shoots all three of them. They seem to be alive as the film ends.

Charlie is a kind of Christ figure, sacrificing himself for his friends. His career chances are ruined. Uncle Johnny will have nothing to do with him; Teresa, should she survive, will pursue her plan to move out of the neighborhood. Johnny Boy is a lost cause. Although he could not abandon them, they may all abandon him.

Thus, the churches, statues, and religious images which recur constantly in the film are not just part of its atmosphere. They are central to the story of a young man determined to *be* grace, to reflect God's love in his care for other humans, however inept and doomed his attempts are. Scorsese, who once studied for the priesthood, sees Charlie as himself and as a priest surrogate. He has not, according to his own admission in interviews and in the confessional work of his art, worked out his struggles with religion (though he is a man of faith), and particularly those which come from the conflict (as he sees it) between faith and sexuality. Yet his desire to be a priest to others and an *alter Christus*, another Christ, continue.

In *The Last Temptation of Christ* he struggled again with the same vocation, convinced as he was that Kazantzakis might contain the solution. The fundamentalists who drove the film out of many theaters missed the point of the film, just as Scorsese himself missed and perhaps still misses the point about both Jesus (who represents God's love, not God's wrath) and sex (which is a sacrament and indeed a Sacrament). The best way to watch the film is to turn off the foolishness of the sound track and revel in the half millennium of Italian and Italian American iconography as it is filtered through the haunted (and at times blood-obsessed) imagination of Martin Scorsese.

Scorsese's (perhaps slightly deviant) Catholic imagination is driven by Catholic images and his work shaped by Catholic pre-occupations about sexuality but also about intimate community. His ambivalence is powerful. To be Catholic is to be guilty, to be "neighborhood" is to be trapped in obligations, to be "family" is a torment. Thus, the fantasies Jesus is presented as having on the Cross, as Lourdeaux wisely notes, are fantasies of community and family with Martha and Mary. They seem to pose as temptations precisely because they represent the appeal of domesticity, of the ordinary, of the limitations on the human spirit imposed by flesh. Martin Scorsese realizes that he cannot escape, any-more than Charlie, the demands of family, neighborhood, and parish.

Is all this typical of Italian Americans only? I wouldn't say that. The Irish have similar problems and possibilities, as I will show in a moment. Scorsese plays brilliantly, and sometimes bizarrely, with the same kinds of problems which assail all of us Catholics who come out of Catholic ethnic communities.

His is perhaps a manic and surely confused analogical imagi-nation, but Catholic it certainly is. One cannot imagine an artist from a Protestant background so obsessed with local community. For writers like Sherwood Anderson or Sinclair Lewis, the solu-tion to one's problems with the local community is simply to move out of Winesburg or Gopher Prairie. The Catholic can never leave the neighborhood behind. Besides, some of the time he doesn't want to.

For an Irish parallel to Scorsese, I turn to the fiction of James T. Farrell, the chronicler of the South Side Chicago Irish.[3] In the era about which Farrell wrote, the turn of the century to the late

1940s, the Irish were in roughly the same social and generational situation as were the Italians in the years when Scorsese was growing up, a time when the second and third generation were struggling for success. The Irish had no mafia—"the Outfit" or "your friends on the West Side" is what we call it in Chicago—and most of their criminality was on the other side of the street, in politics and law enforcement. Otherwise, the cultural environment in and around St. Anselm's at 59th and Indiana was remarkably similar to that of *Mean Streets*, save that the clergy probably had even more power.

Farrell found his neighborhood less attractive than Scorsese does his. Farrell called his classic trilogy *Studs Lonigan* a story of defeat in an environment of spiritual poverty. The spiritual poverty comprised the family, the neighborhood, and the parish, all of which Farrell hated. The books are not about "slum boys," as those who have not read them often think. Studs's family was middle class, his father a painting contractor. His defeat was not caused by the narrow and rigid cultures of his family and community but by the Great Depression, which defeated many other men whose mothers were not as punitive, whose fathers were not as weak, and whose drinking problem was not as great as Studs's.

Sister Liguori Brody, longtime professor of sociology at Mundelein College in Chicago, graduated from the real St. Anselm's the same year the fictional Studs did. She collected data and wrote an essay on "The Classmates of Studs" which examined the lives of those who did not freeze to death in a drunken stupor beneath the L tracks in 1931, leaving their women and unborn children to the mercies of vicious mothers and sisters. (Apparently, Farrell used a real person as the basis for his fictional character.) Unfortunately, the essay was never published.

However, Studs's contemporaries who survived the Great Depression prospered as he would have if the circumstances of his life had been only marginally different. Farrell's point was that the circumstances were bad to begin with, in great part because of his family and his religion. At his time, there was no way out for someone growing up in Washington Park—not that Studs ever seriously sought a way out.

Farrell hated the neighborhood and the parish. He sought new horizons, broader visions, enhanced possibilities. He found them—as did Danny O'Neill, the protagonist of the four volumes of his second series of books—at the University of Chicago.[4] Studs and Danny represent the opposite sides of Farrell in what Charles Fanning has called the Washington Park novels. The former was the Farrell who almost did not escape, the latter the Farrell who just barely escaped—or thought he did. At the university, and later in New York, Farrell found a new life and some initial success as a novelist. However, the fashion in Socialist Realism hardly survived the 1930s, and the critics decided that he was a has-been by the mid-1940s. Now he has become a never-was thanks to that wonderful paragon of cultural diversity, the Modern Language Association, which denies the possibility of panels on his work at their annual meetings.

Farrell continued to write about the neighborhood and the religion he thought he'd left behind with methodical, almost plodding determination. His prose style reminds one of Hemingway without the elegance—a long series of simple declarative sentences unhampered by even a minimum of narrative suspense. Yet he continued to have a wondrous feel for the neighborhood and its people: their hang-ups, their rivalries, their nastiness, their resentments, their long memories, their petty devotions. Moreover he had such a detailed memory of Catholic religious practices of the era of his youth that anyone wanting to do historical research about the Catholic liturgy (a word unknown in the St. Anselm's of Farrell's day) at that time would need only to consult his books. Farrell could no more leave St. Anselm's than Joyce could leave Dublin. From Catholic communities as well as Catholic metaphors there is often no escape. He may not have been a great novelist (there aren't all that many!), but he was a superb participant and observer, a historian and an anthropologist.

Yet in *The Young Studs* he wrote one of the most memorable and lyrical accounts of young love that an American writer has ever produced. The romance between Studs and Lucy Scanlan[5] is more than just a story of puppy love. It is rather a story of possibility, of a different kind of life that is possible without leaving behind the neighborhood. Lucy was not a doomed woman like Charlie's Teresa. She could certainly have resisted the pernicious influence of Studs's mother. She cared for Studs as much as he cared for her. But their attempt to renew their love when they were young adults failed because Studs had become a clumsy drunken boor. There would have been more tragedy in the story if Farrell had given him an honest chance at the new relationship for which Lucy was certainly ready. But the doom Farrell had in mind did not permit even tragedy.

Oddly enough, Farrell's valedictory novel, *The Death of Nora Ryan*, provides a different take on the neighborhood and the religion. Eddie Ryan, one of the successors of Studs and Danny O'Neill, comes back to Chicago for his mother's death and burial. His experiences of his relatives and friends, neighborhood and parish, are almost elegaic. The book received more favorable notices than the critics had given Farrell for a long time. Had he made his peace with St. Anselm's? Had he mellowed? Had he learned the lesson "once a Catholic, always a Catholic"? Or some mix of these three?

Toward the end, Farrell was a fall-down drunk himself. I once received a letter of warm praise from him[6] which was, alas, mostly incoherent, doubtless because the drink had been taken before he wrote it. He also claimed credit for the Second Vatican Council—as much right he as anyone else. At his grave, prayers were recited by a priest from Mount Carmel and a group of younger Catholic scholars who were studying his work.

It is hard to get away from the neighborhood, even when you want to.

Farrell was only one of many Irish American authors who chose neighborhoods and parishes as their setting. Other parochialists were Harry Sylvester in his *Moon Gaffney*, Edwin O'Connor in his Pulitzer-Prize–winning *Edge of Sadness*, William Kennedy in *Ironweed*, J. F. Powers in his short stories, John R. Powers in his *Last Catholic in America*, and Jon Hassler in his Minnesota stories, especially *North of Hope*. The parish has been so important in the life of Irish Catholic immigrants and their children and grandchildren that it would have been impossible to write about them and exclude it. If the tilt among Italian filmmakers is in the direction of the neighborhood aspect of the neighborhood parish, the Irish tilt is toward the parish.

A similar love of the local manifests itself in the artistic production of a much different time and place, in the work of Jan Vermeer, who is preoccupied with his beloved hometown of Delft. His famous painting *The Little Street* sums up the intuition that the houses and the tiny street and the playing child are all that really matters.

The Little Street, by Jan Vermeer.

No one seriously questions that Catholics have always been a community-oriented people. Indeed, the central objection of the Reformers to the Church was precisely that it put a community of humans between the individual soul and God. Classic sociology has depicted the great shift of the late nineteenth century as a turn away from the rural peasant commune to the industrial city, a turn which went on much more slowly in Catholic countries than in Protestant countries. In fact, the classic sociologists argue that the Reformation was in part responsible for the collapse of the old order.

Max Weber saw the constraints of Catholic communalism as inhibiting Catholic educational achievement in early twentieth-century Germany. Emile Durkheim argued that Catholic suicide rates were lower precisely because of Catholic communal constraints against self-destruction. The Catholic self-critics of the 1950s and 1960s, such as Professor John Donovan of Boston College and Monsignor John Tracy Ellis of the Catholic University, agreed that there were no Catholic Salks or Einsteins because the community was a drag on Catholic ambition and achievement. Even today, it is often assumed by sociologists that Catholicism is somehow a barrier to success because of community pressures which make it difficult for Catholics to think for themselves.[7]

Michael Schuck studied the 284 papal encyclicals written between 1740 and 1987 and found that, regardless of context, subject matter, and the personal concerns of various popes, the emphasis has always been on community, whether geographically regional as in the early years or global as in the later years. Indeed, the tradition of papal teachings has, perhaps not altogether consciously, applied the vision of local community to the problems of the world society. In a brilliant summary, Schuck describes the Catholic social ethic:

> Internal to all the popes' social recommendations and judgments is a communitarian understanding of the self and society. Whether rooted in territorial custom, cosmological nature, or affective sentiment, the self is invariably defined by the totality of its relations with other beings and, particularly, with other selves. Hence, the encyclicals constantly protest liberalism's Enlightenment inspired notion of the self as a radically unencumbered, autonomous chooser of ends.
>
> In the papal view, mutuality is a characteristic of embedded selves. This quality, in turn, defines society. Whether construed territorially, cosmologically, or affectively, the notion of society as "koinonia" or community of mutuality "responds to the deepest aspirations of God's human creatures." Concomitantly, all realms of human interaction, religious, political, family, economic, cultural must reflect a "coordinate" interest in mutual aid. Thus, the popes perennially decry the classical liberal model where society is understood as an artificial contract between autonomous individuals "undertaken for self-interested rather than fraternal reasons."

For most of the past two-and-a-half centuries of encyclicals, this worldview would have been considered conservative if not reactionary,[8] a revolt against modernity, a rejection of the "liberal" impulse, a last gasp of a dying order, an order whose death the classic sociologists (particularly Weber) mourned even as they described it. Now it would seem that modernity and individualism are dead (or at least struggling to survive) and the community is fashionable again.

The pertinence of the encyclicals to our discussion is not that the popes have *shaped* Catholic imagination about self and society (though doubtless to some extent they have) but rather that they *reflect* Catholic imagination because they are looking at human life through enchanted Catholic eyes. Their image of society as a network of relationships emerged from their own personal experiences growing up in such networks. No other way of viewing the world made any sense. The "Manchester liberalism" of rugged individualism simply did not fit the experiences of their lives.

Whether Catholics are still communalists remains for the moment an open question. Max Weber himself thought that industrial society would homogenize such differences out of society. Those who believe that the changes recorded by the sociological classics have an inevitable evolutionary thrust seek evidence that differences in worldview based on religion are eroding. Education, mobility, science, technology, the mass media, the world economy, the "secularization" of life, they hold, will eventually eliminate Catholic communalism and indeed have to a considerable extent done so already. The neighborhood, a fading remnant of the peasant village, will be with us only a little while longer. The worlds of Martin Scorsese and James T. Farrell are disappearing.

Yet it remains interesting that, however limited its life expectancy, the neighborhood parish, a peasant community set down in an urban context, should appear in the most advanced industrial society in the world. Dublin doesn't have parishes like Chicago does. Rome, Milan, and Florence don't have neighborhoods like Queens and Brooklyn do.

A number of factors have combined to produce the neighbor-hood parish—large-scale foreign immigration, the tendency of immigrants from similar backgrounds to cluster in the same places in a city, the speed with which organized religion re-sponded to immigrants, the inclination of immigrants to rally around their churches as community centers in the absence of al-ternatives, the resources the local community made available to its members. More abstractly, the neighborhood was a locus for the formation of "social capital," the resources made available to people in a community when membership in networks overlaps. The neighborhood parish was a rational choice for immigrants, although it might have imposed constraints, sometimes harsh, on restless and creative offspring like Scorsese and Farrell.

The neighborhood, with its often intense and sometimes lim-iting relationships, was the place where many Catholic immi-grants worked out their adjustment to urban life in America, the space in which their Catholic view of human networks found an appropriate social form. It enabled them to sustain many of the social patterns they had left behind in their peasant villages while at the same time adjusting to a different society and—as there can be little doubt any more—struggling successfully to become part of that society. For most people throughout most of human history, life in the peasant village was not a matter of choice. But most immigrants to America chose life in the neighborhood. They chose it for its social support and accepted the social con-trol that went with it, especially since the social control proved to be not all that limiting to most of them. The neighborhood was a commune created by (partially) free contract. Most immigrants and their children and grandchildren seem to have liked it. The neighborhood, as Gerald Suttles has remarked, is that place on the urban checkerboard where you matter not because of what you do but because of who you are.[9]

Whether it will disappear or persist, or—as is the case in most human social arrangements—be transformed into something similiar yet new is an empirical question for future sociologists. More pertinent for the present discussion is the question of whether Catholic community ethos persists in the modern industrial world—or, if one believes in such things—the postmodern, post-industrial world. The issue is not whether the neighborhood survives but whether the distinctive Catholic view of human networks which classical sociology described, of which the neighborhood is one manifestation and the papal encyclicals another, survives.

The question may be the most decisive to which this essay addresses itself. There seems to be no debate that Catholicism is a communal religion and that at one time Catholics were different from Protestants in their imagination of human relationships. But are they still different?

There is substantial data to suggest that they have not changed. The International Social Survey Program and the World Values Study have studied human behavior in many countries where there are enough Catholics and Protestants to make fair comparisons. The most crucial of the measures were a series of questions in the 1986 International Social Survey Program research on social networks in which respondents were asked about frequency of contact with family members—parents, siblings, spouses, children—via visits and phone calls as well as residential proximity to those relatives. In all of the countries where comparisons could be made except Hungary— where fear of the government may have caused respondents to downplay their religious ties—there were statistically significant relationships between being Catholic and sustaining close family links.[10] Nor were these correlations diminished by either education or age. Younger Catholics and better-educated Catholics were just as likely to sustain these links as were older Catholics. Finally, in comparisons between the Irish in Ireland with the Irish in America and between Italians in Italy and Italians in America there were in general no significant declines in levels of family interaction.[11] The Irish in both countries were more likely to sustain contact with siblings, the Italians in both countries to sustain contacts with parents. For the Irish there was in fact an increase in phone calls in America, though perhaps only because there are more telephones in America. Italian Americans were as likely as Italians to turn to relatives when they needed short-term help (someone to watch children while one went to the store) or long-term help (a major loan), and both were more likely than anyone else in the countries surveyed. Indeed, the structure of Italian family life, as measured by frequency of contacts, has not been affected by the size of the place in which they live, by education, by age, or by migration to America. Modernity, whatever that may be, has simply not affected the Italian family system. The Irish, for their part, use the telephone (marginally) more often than the Italians to sustain family links. The talk goes on.

Even at the University of Arizona, in the allegedly homogenized Sunbelt, where many students are a long way from home (the second largest enrollment is, not unreasonably, from Illinois), Catholics are more likely than Protestants to phone home or e-mail their parents and siblings. Before I administer the questionnaire, my students tell me that it's silly to think religion will affect these matters. Afterward they tell me that everyone knows that Catholics are more likely to be communal.

One might well wonder why there was any expectation that fundamental family patterns would change, save by those who think that future shock is fact instead of an unproven metaphor. Role expectations are learned very early in life as a child watches adults interact with one another and absorbs tacit templates for appropriate and inappropriate behavior. Just as Catholic images of Mary and Catholic images of sex-as-sacrament are probably passed on to younger generations by families, so are Catholic images of appropriate social networks.

There are other indicators of a Catholic ethos in the International Social Survey Program data. Catholics are less likely than Protestants[12] to support obedience to laws; Catholics are more likely than Protestants to approve violent protests, to support freedom of publication, and to recognize unequal treatment of women; Catholics are less likely than Protestants to resist temporary arrest for suspects and criminals or to feel oppressed by the power structures of society and lack of power in dealing with government. Catholics are less likely than Protestants to think taxes are too high. Catholics are more likely than Protestants to support government intervention in the economy, government ownership of industry, and equalization of income.

The Catholic attitude toward the role of government described in the previous paragraphs may seem paradoxical—more supportive of government intervention and more faith that government is a positive good, yet also more likely to take to the streets in protest when the flaws of government become intolerable. Catholic theologians like Thomas Aquinas approved of tyrannicide in certain circumstances. Martin Luther disagreed.

Catholics and Protestants, then, have different models, templates, paradigms, images, metaphors to shape their attitudes and behavior in both familial and societal relationships. There is no evidence that either youthfulness or education diminish these differences.

The liberal/conservative paradigm cannot cope with the Catholic propensity to support liberal policies on government intervention and egalitarianism and conservative policies in response to crime. However, a paradigm based on a theory of different "imaginations" (or "ethics") can easily account for the patterns reported: under ordinary circumstances, Catholics tend to picture society as supportive and not oppressive, while Protestants tend to picture society as oppressive and not supportive. The latter take oppression for granted: it goes with the territory. The former do not: while they expect the government to provide protection from crime, they are willing to go into the street when the government fails in its larger obligations to serve the people.

Turning to the five English-speaking countries[13] in the European Values Study, one finds that similar patterns emerged: in all five countries, Catholics are more likely to emphasize "fairness" and "equality," while Protestants are more likely to emphasize "freedom" and "individualism" in the workplace. With the exception of those in Great Britain, Catholics are also more likely to advocate strengthening of authority and of the family. And in the United States and Ireland, they are also more likely to say that if they didn't have to work five days a week they would devote themselves to the community and/or to a small business of their own. Catholics are localists.

In all five countries, Catholics are more willing than Protestants to accept political extremists of either the left or the right into their neighborhoods. With the exception of Australia, they are also more likely to accept those with drinking and emotional problems. (This is probably because alcoholism is a more acute problem in Australia than in the other countries surveyed—but explanations of exceptions are beyond the scope of this book.)

In Ireland and Australia, and to some extent in Canada (though not in the United States and Great Britain), Catholics are more likely than Protestants to have strong positions on issues of "life ethics": abortion, extramarital sex, euthanasia, suicide, and so on. In all five countries, Protestants are more likely than Catholics to emphasize issues of "personal ethics": lying, cheating, stealing, bribing. In all the countries but the United States, Catholics are more likely than Protestants to disapprove of "socially disruptive" behavior such as joyriding, union busting, fighting with police, and failing to report damage to another's car. Catholics tend to communalism in their ethical concerns, Protestants to individualism.

In all five countries, Catholics are more likely than Protestants to report agreement on crucial issues with parents and spouses and to emphasize the importance of shared backgrounds (religion, politics, tastes) as conditions for successful marriage. Protestants are more likely than Catholics to insist on the importance of sexual fulfillment and on living apart from parents and in-laws as conditions for a successful marriage. Thus, Catholics are more likely than Protestants to see marriage in a social context.

In the countries studied, Protestants were more likely to value industry and thrift in their children and Catholics more likely to value religious faith and a sense of loyalty and duty (with the exception of Ireland, where Protestants rate loyalty and duty higher than do Catholics, perhaps because of the special circumstances in Northern Ireland). Finally, in all five countries Catholics are more likely than Protestants to emphasize traditional family values, and in all countries but Ireland, Protestants are more likely than Catholics to be tolerant of "sexual revolution" behavior. (In contrast, International Social Survey Program data show that Ireland—all twenty-six Republican counties—and the Netherlands are the most likely to be tolerant of homosexual marriages, as in fact are Irish Americans. No model fits perfectly.)

Modern empirical social science emerged at a moment when change from an "old order" to a "new order" in Europe was everywhere to be observed, a change already far along according to the founding fathers of sociology. The "mechanical" society was replacing the "organic" society, "*Gesellschaft*" was replacing "*Gemeinschaft*," "association" was replacing "community." The Protestant ethic, broadly defined as the "individualist" ethic, was replacing the Catholic ethic, broadly defined as the "communal" ethic.

Since the end of the Second World War, scholars have refined and lent nuance to that vision, concluding that, while change has occurred and continues to occur, its development is far more complex, uneven, and multidimensional than it appeared to be a hundred years ago.

Despite contemporary sophistication about the evolutionary changes which the classical sociologists noted, there still is often a moment of surprise when one finds that, in yet another matter, the archaic communal values manage to survive, especially when that matter is religious. Ought not the Catholic ethic, clearly a relic of earlier, less industrialized times, gradually erode in the face of the irresistible forces of individualism and social and geographic mobility? How does one account for the residual strength of this supposedly outmoded worldview? How does an ethical orientation rooted in an agricultural and feudal history manage to survive in an utterly different, hypermodern environment?

The answer seems to be that worldviews are not propositional paragraphs that can be explicated and critiqued in discursive fashion. Rather they are, in their origins and in their primal power, tenacious and durable narrative symbols that take possession of the imagination early in the socialization process and provide patterns which shape the rest of life. These patterns are encoded in different stories of God's relationships with the world and with humankind. In one story, God relates to us as free and independent but isolated individuals, in the other as members of integrated social and communal networks.

How does all this matter? Surely, the Catholic imagination of community is useful for more than setting patterns for human relationships—patterns which, like all else human, are often both good and bad. Since Protestants are satisfied on the average with being individualists and Catholics on the average are satisfied with being communualists, why bother about these differences in their imaginative frameworks?

One answer to this question comes from the work of University of Chicago sociologist Anthony Bryk and his colleagues in their book *Catholic Schools and the Common Good*. Previously, James Coleman and I had both found independently that students in Catholic high schools had higher scores on standardized achievement tests than students in other high schools. We also discovered that the higher scores at Catholic high schools were heavily concentrated among students who had been disadvantaged by previous educational experiences, disciplinary or emotional problems, psychological strain from family life, or lack of family educational background. Furthermore, the more the disadvantages piled one on another, the more successful the Catholic schools were in helping them. The net result was that minority students did better in Catholic high schools. Then Coleman, his colleagues, and I settled finally the issue of whether this was because they came from more motivated families by showing that even holding constant sophomore scores, the students in Catholic high schools had higher senior scores in math and English.[14]

Now, using complicated mathematical models developed for the project, Bryk and his colleagues found three explanations for this startling success of Catholic high schools:

1. Their academic demands were greater; in particular, the schools demanded more courses in English and math.

2. They gave more personal attention to the individual student.

3. They enjoyed more community support both for the student and for the other members of the school community.

Thus, the Catholic social ethos was alive and well and working to the benefit of the minority and disadvantaged[15] student. It was not only a specifically Catholic way of looking at reality, it was also a resource—a resource which, incidentally, is not available, according to the data, in church-related schools which are not Catholic. (Catholics have always advertised the benefits of their communalism on eductional outcome, but without any proof until now.) Catholics administer their schools and teach in them the way one would expect communualists to approach education.

Just as the Catholic sacramental style shapes Catholics in their liturgy to make them more interested in fine arts, so the Catholic communal style shapes the kind of education Catholics provide in their schools.

No doubt, both of these shaping processes work unselfconsciously. They were simply the way things were done, and still are. Catholic high schools, like all high schools, are far from perfect, just as Catholic liturgies are far from perfect. Yet with all their imperfections, they still show some impact of the Catholic sensibility on ordinary life today, even if most Catholics, including Catholic leaders, are unaware of their existence.

CHAPTER FIVE

Hierarchy

N ormally, three distinguishing characteristics are associated with Catholicism: sacramentality, community, and hierarchy. Catholicism believes in metaphors, communal relationship to the Deity, and leadership organized in ascending layers of authority and power. I prefer the word "structure" to "hierarchy" because the latter suggests that the present relationship between pope and bishops, and among bishops and clergy and people, is a given. Anyone who knows Catholic history knows that for most of it—indeed, until the beginning of the present century—bishops were elected by clergy and laity, and that for the first thousand years and more the papacy's control of local dioceses was tenuous at best. There has always been strong leadership in the Church, and bishops were always the local leaders and were responsible in some fashion to the pope, but it is only since the advent of modern communications and transportation with the transatlantic cable, and steam liner that

OPPOSITE: A priest blessing a shrimping fleet in Delcambre, Louisiana. Photo by Philip Gould, courtesy CORBIS.

the present close supervision of local bishops by Rome has been a possibility. Whether these innovations are good for the Church is an issue which is beyond the scope of the present essay. Catholicism has always been hierarchial, and the effects of modern technology on its style of leadership are only the most recent in a series of changes spanning its long history.

I use the word "structure" (established patterns of behavior with supporting motivations) because the Catholic imagination has always recognized that the community is structured. Structure implies organization, which is not possible without leadership, which in turn requires hierarchy. In other words, hierarchy exists as a necessary component of any organized community. The Church is not a chaotic mass of independent individuals but an ordered community in which diversity pervades both leadership and membership. It is the image of organized community that affects the Catholic imagination rather than the more narrow phenomenon of ordered leadership, which is a means to the end of organization. Hierarchy is implicit in the notion of community because without leadership community soon descends into anarchy.

"Catholicism" may well mean "Here Comes Everybody," but everyone comes not as part of a rush of independent actors who descend pell-mell on the community but rather as a member of a preexisting subcommunity. American Catholicism assumed it would deal with new waves of immigrants by responding to them not as a mass of undifferentiated new Americans but as members of specific ethnic groups.

Irish novelist James Joyce illustrates as well as anyone the Catholic sensibility's passion for organization. This may at first seem a bizarre claim: if there is any writing in the English lan-

guage which is disorganized and confusing, it is Joyce's. Granted
that the meaning in his three major works grows increasingly
opaque, Joyce still organizes his stories around rigid time and
space patterns: a day in Dublin in 1904; a night in a hotel and
pub in Capelizod, a quasi-suburb on the west side of Dublin,
probably in the late 1930s.[1]

David Tracy, in an as yet unpublished analysis of the varieties
of Catholic imagination, offers a brilliant analysis of the Irish
Catholic variety. Its experience of the spiritual, he suggests, is essentially simple in that it encounters the transcendent in ordinary experiences of nature—land, water, trees, birds, animals,
the seasons of the year. However, because it is an Irish experience, the telling of it must be convoluted, intricate, and above all
exuberantly playful. The story must be at the same time fantastic
and structured—otherwise it is not playful. Tracy cites the Book
of Kells[2] as the classic example of Irish play—that is, structured
fantasy which often shows little regard for the principle of con-
tradiction. It is worth noting, Tracy observes, that Joyce carried
a copy of the Book of Kells wherever he wandered, perhaps sensing that he was playing the same game of carefully structured,
exuberantly playful fantasy—the Irish Catholic imagination,
perhaps, pushed to its ultimate level of luxuriance.

Ulysses is organized around a specific day in Dublin and indeed around the geographical map of the city. It has been argued
that, having never been to Dublin, one might still draw a map of
the city after a careful reading of the novel. After one has read
Ulysses and made the required Bloomsday pilgrimage, the city
never quite seems the same—another layer of magic has been
added to its already multilayered enchantment. Not trusting his
memory, Joyce was obsessive about seeking precise details about

the structure of the city from Irish visitors whom he encountered during his long exile. In a very real sense, he never left Dublin because his imagination was always there.

This passion for not merely a place but an organized and ordered place was, I would argue, not just an obsession for Joyce; it was absolutely essential to his creative work. Dublin was not only the setting for his story but also a major character in it, and he had no choice but to get the city right. Without the structure Dublin afforded his fantasy, he could not write it.

In this respect—as in so many others, and perhaps without realizing it—Joyce was profoundly Catholic. He needed not only to love Dublin—and hate it, too, but with more of the former than the latter—he had to describe precisely its special configuration. He could, for example, imagine the wild adventures in Night Town only when he was sure he had told the reader where that now legendary Dublin neighborhood was and what it was like.

As Seamus Heaney would remark later (without having Joyce particularly in mind), sense of place for the Irish is the combination of a physical place with an overlay of meaning. Without the place, no overlay. For a certain kind of Catholic sensibility, if there is no "real" place, there can be no meaning.

And the place must always be part of another place. It is not enough to say of the shrine of Mamene (restored by my colleague and friend Micheal McGriel) that it is in the Montauk Mountains. One must add that it is on the border between Galway and Mayo—in Celtic lands, borders are sacred and hence both dangerous and promising. One can read many Catholic novels and see many Catholic films and not fully understand them until one realizes that the setting is not only background but also a character in the story, a structured place which is part of a larger structure and which imposes its order not only on the other characters but also on the story itself—not to mention the reader.

It is in the nature of community that it be ordered. Even a poker club which meets every other week is likely to distribute duties—bringing the cards or the chips or the beer. If the community is big enough, it may have many layers of order and hence even "hierarchy," in the most elementary sense of that word. Even a family is likely to devolve elements of its power to various members. Women generally are the cooks, though in this day of changing gender roles, some men usurp this role traditionally associated with women's power. Women also are generally in charge of hurt feelings and sensitivities. Thus, the notion that one can have a religious community in which all are absolutely equal, however appealing it may be, is difficult if not impossible to achieve in practice. As the pigs say in George Orwell's *Animal Farm*, some animals are more equal than others. The difference between the Catholic religious sensibility and the Protestant one with regard to communal religious structure is that the latter tends to see power as evil and human nature as perverted by it.[3] The Catholic religious sensibility, while alert to the abuse of authority, tends to feel that authority in itself is not evil and that order in a community is essential. It accepts a structured and diversified community, whether James Joyce's Dublin or Richard Daley's Chicago.

Protestant denominations do not lack structure or power centers, but they shift the emphasis of their rhetoric in an attempt to downplay that power. As Paul Harrison pointed out in his classic work, *Authority in the Free Church Tradition*, the denominational bureaucracies must present themselves as speaking *to* the church instead of *for* it. But bureaucratic power is bureaucratic power, no matter what mask it wears: it is both absolutely essential in any large organization, and it is also open to abuse. Interestingly, Catholics who are members of a Church which is admittedly hierarchial (regrettably, perhaps, now more than ever) and frequently authoritarian are much less likely than Southern Baptists, members of an allegedly free church, to insist on the importance of the teachings of church leaders. Perhaps an acknowledged religious bureaucracy has less power than an unacknowledged one.[4]

A dimension of this Catholic acceptance of the need for order is the conviction that the most effective order is that which reaches directly into the community in which it is emerging, and where the people whose cooperation will be necessary for the implementation of a decision will be most likely to have an input into the making of that decision. Rather than accept the adage which holds that the best government is the one which governs least, the Catholic imagination would rather say, paraphrasing Tip O'Neill, that the best government is that which is the most local. In a properly ordered society, nothing is done at a higher level which can be done just as well at a lower level—thus holds the principle of subsidiarity.[5] This image of society as an organized community—or better yet, an organized community of organized communities—is not one that either centralizing capitalism or centralized socialism likes. It doesn't sound very efficient. Big and centrally controlled is efficient, small and locally controlled is not. The Catholic imagination knows better.[6] Small is both more human and more efficient.

The Catholic Church preaches this principle to other human organizations, but it is distinctly ambivalent about practicing it itself. Indeed, some Vatican theologians argue that the principle does not in fact apply to the Church because of the Church's "divine origin," an argument which is like saying that Jesus did not sweat. Nevertheless, whether because of latent subsidiarity or incompetence, the Church is not very good at micromanaging what goes on in the local parish, which for most Catholics is where the Church is. Particularly in the years since the Second Vatican Council, which increasingly have seen a "seller's market" for parish pastors, de facto subsidiarity flourishes in the Catholic Church.

Can one test this Catholic image of ordered community against empirical data? I know of no data which measure Catholic attitudes either toward ordered community or decentralization of power. An International Social Survey module on national identity, whose questions were asked in 1995, provides information on attitudes toward respondents' own localities, toward the world, and toward immigrants. One would predict on the basis of my preceding argument that Catholics would be more likely to feel close to their own locales but also, because of their image of society as a network of structures, to the world beyond. One would also expect them to be more tolerant of immigrants.

In fact all of these expectations are supported. Four questions ask about how close a respondent feels to neighborhood, county,[7] and continent. The four items form a factor, or a cluster of related responses. Catholics score significantly higher than Protestants, with the largest differences appearing in their attitudes toward neighborhood and continent. On a scale measuring attitudes toward immigrants and crime, immigrants and the economy, and immigrants and jobs, Catholics are significantly more likely to be sympathetic to immigrants than are Protestants. This paradigm linking local and global concerns is also found in the encyclicals of the current papacy, especially as analyzed by Schuck: it reveals an imagination which sees the world as a community of communities, Joyce's Dublin writ large.

In other International Social Survey Program data, Catholics are more likely to support government intervention to equalize wages, which suggests a support for orderly restraints instead of rugged individualistic competition. Yet in the American General Social Survey, the attitudes of Catholics toward AIDS, racism, feminism, civil liberties, trust of others, militarism, the environment, and the ownership of weapons tended to support the side of freedom and compassion.

These findings, which surely were not what the researchers expected, illustrate a problem with reporting the hard facts about Catholic social attitudes. Everyone from Pat Buchanan to the editorial writers of the *Washington Post* and the *New York Times* knows that Catholics are social conservatives, especially on issues of family, sex, and abortion. Therefore, it is impossible that they would be more sympathetic than Protestants to AIDS victims or to feminism, and it follows that such findings should simply be dismissed.

The reality is that, on most such issues, Catholics are less liberal than Jews and those with no religious affiliation, but more liberal than Protestants. Since Jews and those with no religious affiliation are less than 10 percent of American society and Catholics are about 25 percent, Catholics are patently on the liberal end of the political spectrum and always have been. In a recent analysis of voting patterns, Brooks and Manza (1997) have confirmed that Catholics have not drifted away disproportionately from Democratic voting patterns in presidential elections since 1952. Taking into account the changes in voting patterns which are peculiar to each presidential election, such as the swings toward Eisenhower in the 1950s and toward Clinton in the 1990s, Catholics are as likely to vote for the Democratic candidate as they were a half century ago.

Why does conventional wisdom continue to hold that Catholics are political conservatives despite empirical evidence of which Manza and Brooks's is only the most recent and methodologically sophisticated? One might expect this prejudice of a Pat Buchanan, but why has it also engulfed the academy and the national media? This anti-Catholic prejudice has become truth beyond dispute because both "conservatives" and "liberals" want it to be true—the former because they would like to believe that Catholics are part of their coalition, and the latter because they don't want Catholics in their coalition.

Thus, whether anyone on either end of the political spectrum likes it or not, and consistent with the Catholic image of an ordered community in which there must be concern for all members, American Catholics are more likely to support civil liberties (the right of a Communist or atheist to speak), to oppose militarism (more money for arms), to support gun control and not to own guns themselves, to support greater environmental efforts, and to trust other people. Moreover, each of these attitudes and behaviors correlates positively with Catholic scores on the Grace Scale and negatively or not at all with Protestant Grace scores. In short, the more Catholic their imagination, the more likely Catholics are to respond with attitudes which are compatible with the image of human groups as structured and ordered communities. But order exists to facilitate freedom, not to diminish

it. American imagery, arising as it does out of puritan individualism, considers order and freedom to be contradictory; the
Catholic notion of community sees them as complementary.

I speculate that this Catholic "liberalism" is not the ideological liberalism of most Americans who think of themselves as liberal. It is not based on any compulsion to make everyone immediately equal to everyone else, or to impose virtue on a society
which is perceived as lacking in virtue. Rather, it results from a
kind of sympathetic pragmatism, a sense that no group of members of a human community should be excluded, lest the structure of the community become oppressive and malign.

This speculation is confirmed by European Values Study data
which shows that, of the English-speaking peoples, the Irish are
the most likely to tolerate diverse groups as their neighbors
(drunks, radicals, immigrants, students, left-wing radicals, right-
wing radicals, etc.), and they are the most likely to be tolerant of
diversity precisely because they are Catholic. To put the matter
differently, if the other English-speaking countries had the same
proportion of Catholics as does Ireland, then there would be no
differences among them in tolerance of diversity.

In the Catholic sensibility, you cannot have community without order, and that order requires you to respect all the diverse
people that are part of it. Such a sensibility is not overwhelming
enough to make American Catholics very different from American Protestants, but it does make them somewhat different,
which is all this essay's central theory claims.

Very well, you might argue, I have established that the Catholic imagination pictures communities as structured and organized, as communities of subcommunities. I have contended
that, because they recognize the validity of other subcommuni-

ties, Catholics are more concerned about respect for communities other than their own. I have subsumed hierarchy under structure. But I have not faced the fact that hierarchy can be oppressive and has often been so within Catholicism. I must deal with that fact before I can persuade you that, at least at the imaginative level, hierarchy can be and often is benign.

Fair enough. To respond, I will turn to that hierarchial relationship which is the only one most laypeople encounter, that with their parish clergy. The chancery office is downtown, the Vatican is in Rome—both are a long way off. The parish priest is right down the street. I contend that the laity react to their parish priests, both in art and in real life, with a mixture of respect for their role and tolerance of their humanity.

Why is the world fascinated by priests? Why, from *The Thornbirds* to *Priest*, from *The Power and the Glory* to *The Edge of Sadness*, from Father Brown to Bishop Blackie, have priests been objects of fascination? Why do priests seem to be marked men, even if often they don't want to be? The answer, I believe, is that they *are* marked, if not theologically, then at least sociologically. Once a Catholic, always a Catholic. Once a priest, always a priest.

In the Catholic tradition, the priest is more than merely a preacher of the word. He is a sacrament. When he presides over the Eucharist, he stands in the role of Jesus the high priest and is touched therefore lightly but permanently by the transcendent. This role demands of him special efforts at goodness, despite his ordinary human fragility. Catholics are well aware of this duality in the priestly role. It is imprinted on their religious imagination from their earliest years that the priest is human like everyone else, yet someone special. He is the sacramental center of the

Catholic community and of Catholic worship. Yet, as the author of the Epistle to the Hebrews writes, the priest is taken from among humans so that his awareness of his own human weakness can help him understand the problems of his fellow humans.

In the old days, the comment "Poor Father isn't feeling very well this morning" meant that poor Father was drunk again. Catholics have realized all along that priests can be drunkards, loafers, tyrants, liars, thieves, and, worst of all, rotten preachers. More recently, the Catholic laity has realized that priests can also violate their vows of celibacy and even be sexual predators. Many laypeople know, or know of, a priest who has died of AIDS. None of this affects either their Catholic faith or their respect for the priesthood, as a *Boston Globe* poll showed at the time of the Father Porter case in Massachusetts, in which a priest abused hundreds of children. Catholics no longer feel the need to deny or to hide these truths, despite the anti-Catholic sentiments they sometimes engender, in part because they know that other denominations have the same problems and in part because they are now secure in being both Catholic and American.

There is no room for the cult of personality in the Catholic tradition, unless the personalities are in heaven (Jesus, Mary, the saints, and the angels). Catholicism recognizes no sacred persons, not priests, not bishops, not mothers superior, not even popes. There are sacred functional roles in Catholicism, and the individuals who fulfill these roles are entitled to respect—but worship, not one bit. The cult of the pope, promoted by the Curia and, alas, by many Catholic teachers, began only in the middle of the last century and is utterly inappropriate—especially considering some of the men who have been popes in the distant past (and some in the not-so-distant past). Pope John

Paul II has said that the title "Vicar of Christ" is not theologically appropriate but must be tolerated as custom. It would be much better if it were not tolerated. Popes may be good and holy men, but they are not God. Like the rest of us, they have limitations and imperfections (some of them serious) and make mistakes (some of them serious, too).

There is little Catholic literature about popes—save for the wonderful novels of Morris West—and not much about cardinals or bishops, either. (Cardinal Frederigo Borromeo in Manzoni's *I Promissi Sposi* is a striking exception.) But there is a vast literature about the occupants of the truly most important functional role in Catholicism, the role which is most efficacious in representing the hierarchy among ordinary people—that of the priest. Most of the authors have got it right, too: the priest is anything but sacred—often, he is anything but holy—but he is important for what he does. However ineptly, he presides over the Eucharistic community and preaches the Word. He is human like everyone else, not necessarily better than anyone else and yet . . . and yet . . . because he does what he does, he must strive more than others to be good, and perhaps what he does sets for him a trajectory toward that end.

Graham Greene had it exactly right in his novel *The Power and the Glory* (and John Ford's film, *The Fugitive*, which fudged to keep the Catholic Legion of Decency happy, had it precisely wrong). The whiskey priest is a weak and sinful man, a drunk and a lecher and a coward. And yet . . . and yet . . . the glory of the priesthood—the dignity of the role this unworthy man occupies—overwhelms his weakness and makes him a martyr and a saint. Any priest who does not feel that he is a weak man driven to virtue of which he is not really capable by the power

An audience with Pope John XXIII. Photo by David Lees, courtesy CORBIS.

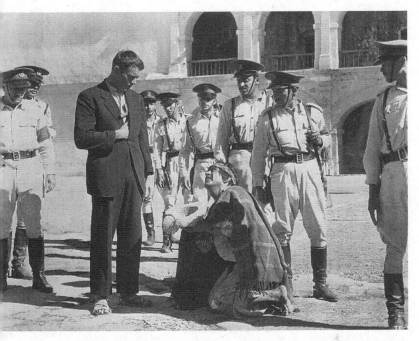

Henry Fonda (standing, left of center) in John Ford's *The Fugitive*.

and the glory of his sacred function is grossly deficient in self-awareness.

Arguably, *The Power and the Glory* is the best book about the Catholic priesthood ever written. All the more ironic, then, that Rome condemned it—not publicly so it would make the publisher's day, but privately. In his preface to the book in the uniform series, Greene tells how he was summoned to Westminster by the cardinal archbishop and constrained to listen to a very embarrassed cardinal read the Roman letter of condemnation.

Why did the book deserve condemnation? Because it portrayed a priest who was a sinner! Somehow, the curial dicasteries had missed the point that at the end, precisely because of his function in the Church, he became a saint.

In ages past, other Catholic authors encountered no such condemnation. No one had to pretend that, since priests were sacred persons, they could do no wrong. On the contrary, this near heresy is a recent phenomenon associated most notoriously with scandals resulting from the Church's foolish attempt to cover up for sex-abusing priests. Consider four friars—Chaucer's Friar, Shakespeare's Friar Lawrence, Robin Hood's Friar Tuck, and Manzoni's Friar Christofero, each of them presumably a follower of St. Francis of Assisi. Four utterly different priests. The first a smooth operator, the second a good and gentle man who did the best he could for the two star-crossed lovers, the third a roistering and vulgar fighter who was nonetheless on the side of the poor and the oppressed, and the fourth, a saintly man who also tried to help star-crossed lovers and died of the plague. Not a bad quartet all in all, all thoroughly human, and each of them to some extent driven by their vocation to become something more than they are.

Manzoni's novel is less about the fidelity of Renzo and Lucia, who often seem mere stick figures created to make a point, than it is about three priests, the friar, the parish priest (Don Albondio), and Cardinal Borromeo of Milan—the first a simple saint, the second a coward and conniver, and the third a towering giant of wisdom and fortitude.[8] Some priests are saints, some are sinners, and most of us are in between. Catholics do not expect perfect men as priests, but they like it when they encounter good men who are also good at their work.

Two American Catholic writers were not afraid to describe priests warts and all—Edwin O'Connor in his classic Pulitzer Prize winner, *The Edge of Sadness*, and J. F. Powers in his short stories and especially in his novel *Morte D'Urban*. Father Hugh Kennedy is the real protagonist of *Edge*, a man who is far from perfect and is at best a marginally good priest who drinks too much. And yet the power and the glory of the priesthood will not leave him alone. He becomes nothing like a saint as the story goes on but certainly a very good priest. Father Urban is an ecclesiastical operator par excellence, which means that he is not really all that skillful an operator (and perhaps not unlike Chaucer's friar). Yet at the end he undergoes a *metanoia*, too, and becomes much more appealing as a priest. It would almost seem that writers like O'Connor, Powers, and Greene, knowing full well the weakness of the clergy, nonetheless want to see their priest protagonists yield themselves over to the power and the glory which lurks like an aura around them. They are poor metaphors for God's love, but metaphors just the same.

Studies of the attitudes of the laity toward their priests suggest that the people in the pews are realists about their clergy. They find their preaching, their counseling, and their respect for women woefully inadequate, but they still think their pastor is doing a good job (by which they probably mean he is a good administrator or tries to be one) and that he means well. Half of them would still be greatly pleased if their son should choose to be a priest—this figure down only 10 percent since the early 1960s, before the vast changes caused by the Second Vatican Council.

Elite Catholic journalists and academics often decry the image of the priest created by Bing Crosby and Pat O'Brien in the old films and celebrate its replacement by more realistic images such as those, for example, in the film *Priest*.[9] However, the problem with that salacious and scabrous film, created by viciously angry "fallen away" Catholics, is not that the pastor is sleeping with the housekeeper, or that the curate is an active gay, or that the bishop is a cruel fool: all such situations do happen, perhaps on rare occasion in the same rectory. The problem with *Priest* is that it condemns the gay priest for not violating the seal of confession of the abused young woman and yet does not acknowledge[10] that, as soon as the girl's abusing father comes into the confessional to brag about his abuse (not to confess it), every priest in the world would feel free to call the police.

Did *Priest* shake any Catholic's faith in the church? Did it trouble anyone's image of priests? Did it horrify anyone who was not horrified by the stories of sexual abuse? I very much doubt it.[11]

Three research analyses in which I have engaged support the notion that the priest is still a sacrament for Catholics. In the first I investigated the impact on a marriage if the woman had a confidant relationship with a priest. The finding was that such a relationship contributed to a greater propensity for her to report that her marital satisfaction was "excellent" and a similar propensity for her husband. Her relationship with the priest confidant—a man she can trust, but still a man—perhaps enhances her self-image and makes her a more confident lover with her husband. Husbands and wives in such relationships were also more likely to support both celibacy for the clergy and the ordination of women, perhaps because at some level of consciousness they sought such a confidante for husbands. No such correlations existed for Protestants in a confidant relationship with a member of their clergy.

In a second study, I found that a confidant relationship also helped a woman to remain a practicing Catholic when her feminist principles were at odds with the image of a woman's role she had acquired from her mother. No such relationship existed for relationships with Protestant clergy.

Finally, young people who had engaged in a conversation with a priest during the previous year and who some time before that had been at odds with the Church were more likely to return to the Church than those who had no such conversation.

Sacraments, signs of God's presence in the world that they are, priests are enchanted men—often even when they don't want to be.

Catholics in the United States today, then, are as simultaneously realistic and idealistic about their priests as are the authors who created classic Catholic examples of priests in their stories. They accept the fact that those who occupy a role which makes them metaphors for Christ are human, and yet they expect more from them because of that role—and sometimes get it. Their most serious complaint is about the quality of priestly preaching, a complaint somehow voiced by all Catholics yet heard by very few priests. The whiskey priest in the *Power and the Glory* and the two priests in Georges Bernanos's novels *Diary of a Country Priest* and *Under the Sun of Satan* were not good preachers, either. The first was a drunk and a coward, the other two were stupid and inept. The first, however, was also a martyr, the second a man who saw grace everywhere, and the third[12] a worker of miracles (though against his own will). In lieu of good preaching, American Catholics would settle, I suspect, for martyrdom, grace, and miracles. However, all the evidence shows that they have no fewer illusions about the perfection of priests as sacred persons than do Greene, Powers, O'Connor, Hassler, or Bernanos. Nor do they have any illusions about the power and the glory of the priesthood which inheres somehow in the most unappealing of priests.

They would also be happy with a priest like those portrayed by Pat O'Brien or Bing Crosby or like the contemporary Father Ray in *Nothing Sacred*, especially if he were as decent a preacher as they all were.

The Catholic religious imagination, therefore, is not simply communal. It perceives communities as organized networks of subcommunities all of which are worthy of equal respect. Finally, it sees hierarchy as necessary to community structure, especially that local level of hierarchy which the parish clergy represents. Catholicism, for all its global commitment, is a profoundly local religion. If all politics, pace Tip O'Neill, are local, so too is all religion and all religious hierarchy. A Catholic may wish that the pope ruled differently or that the bishop was more open to other points of view. But the man who really counts in her life is the local priest, a man about whom she has no illusions, but to whom she always looks as a sacrament of hope.

CHAPTER SIX

Salvation

T he slow movement of Mozart's Piano Concerto no. 26 is one of the saddest musical compositions ever written. The composer's career was in jeopardy. His work was no longer as popular as it had been. His health was poor, his marriage deeply troubled, his spirit uneasy. His genius, it seemed, had worn out its welcome. He lived on the margin of failure. He did not have much longer to live, though there is no way he could have known that. But he had to face the possibility that he was a "has-been."

Mozart felt with reason that his enormous talent was unappreciated, but he was too busy to indulge in melancholy moods. He was certainly not paralyzed by self-pity, much less prolonged melancholy; he couldn't afford to be. He had to keep on working simply to pay his bills. So the profound sadness of the concerto, particularly in the exquisite slow movement, is mysterious, a revelation of an aspect of Mozart's personality that we rarely

OPPOSITE: *Christ Carrying the Cross*, by Gian Francesco de Maineri. Courtesy CORBIS/Arte & Immagini.

encounter in his music, a glimpse into an obscure corner of his soul. We know that he heard the melodies in his head and wrote them down as he heard them, often as fast as his fingers could move. For all the disappointments and frustrations of his life, sadness rarely entered his melodies. Perhaps he was to busy staying alive to realize how sad he often was.

What was the cause of the underlying sadness which slipped to the surface of this concerto? His dependence on unpredictable patrons? His awareness that his compositions were not fulfilling the promise of his talent because he was writing to the specifications of others and not to his own creative impulses? The rudeness of those who talked while his music was being played? The fact that his father didn't love him?

Perhaps he was sad for all of these reasons, perhaps for none of them. It is more likely he was sad because his musical gift brought him to the ultimate limit of human achievement and then stopped there. Even at the best of times, he had a sense that the very best of his creative work was not good enough. The criteria determining what was good were not the standards of his fickle patrons, but his own. Even the most beautiful work fell short of what he wanted. He came close to touching perfection and did not quite make it—and he was the greatest musician who ever lived, indeed, perhaps the greatest genius who ever lived. Like all of us, he hungered for the absolute and did not quite reach it. Like most of us (excepting those haunted—obsessed— by God), he may have been consciously aware of this failure only when everything else seemed to fail, too. The God-haunted think they are failures all the time.

The music of the concerto is sad, but not despairing. Unlike Wagner, Mozart does not rail or rebel. In his sadness there is also a hint of wit, of self-ridicule, of a sense that like all other things, the sadness too will pass. Hence, the sadness of the concerto is not terrifying, not inconsolable, not unbearable. Rather, because it is Mozart's sorrow, it is elegant, graceful, somehow reassuring. It is a sadness at the disappointments of life which accepts those disappointments with a rueful tear but also—in the very beauty with which the sadness is expressed—with a trace of hope. One listens to the music and says, I have felt that way many times as I realize how fragile and tenuous life is, how close I am at every minute to being cast back into the nothingness from which I came. Mozart has expressed the sorrow for me so I can recognize it in my own experience and face my own fragility, my own mortality, my own perplexing limitations. In that recognition I find hope, as perhaps he did.

Did Mozart smile when he dashed off that haunting melody? Smile at himself, despite his tears, sensing that beauty was stronger than tears and would eventually triumph over the perplexing limitations of the human life?

The Catholic sensibility, I suggest, finds grace in limitation, fragility, mortality. It comes up against the wall of perplexity which surrounds our condition and backs away, sad but hopeful because it strongly suspects there is something beyond that wall.

In that most romantic of operas, *La Traviata*, Verdi touches on the same silver lining of human experience—salvation through sadness and the sacrament of hope. Poor, doomed Violetta forgives Alfredo and Germond, and they forgive one another. She promises her lover a happy life in which he will never forget her love but be freed by it to love another. It's all very sad, but innocent of despair. Violetta has made her peace with everyone (including God, especially if one sees a version of it in which

the clergy visit her in the final act). Her lover and his father realize that they have been irrevocably blessed by her, and she ex-
pires not only saved but also victorious. The audience experiences the same mix of sadness and hope that Mozart's concerto
can create for those who listen to it carefully.

Mozart and Verdi are telling us stories of salvation, of tragedy
and hope, of the grace that is pervasive even in grief. Did they realize that they were disclosing grace, that they were writing
music which was inherently sacramental because it revealed
whatever it is that lurks beyond the wall of perplexity and also is
somehow present in the beauty of the music?

I suspect they did not. They were simply composing, but they
were composing as men possessing and possessed by a religious
imagination which sensed that enchantment is everywhere, even
in sadness. Charles-François Gounod, sometime seminarian,
lifelong theologian, probably had a clearer idea of what he was
doing when he had his angels snatch Margarita off triumphantly
into heaven to leave Faust on his knees, pondering his own fate.
Faust had resisted the limitations of life; he had rejected perplexity; he had rebelled against his own frailty. Now he must pay the
price.

Or must he? In some versions of the Faust story, he, too, finds
salvation. He, too, is overwhelmed by grace, saved by Margarita's
forgiving love, just as Alfredo is saved by Violetta's love. Whatever Gounod's intent was (and I suspect he destined Faust for
damnation, as Mozart did Don Giovanni), he was willing to leave
the decision to God. The Catholic imagination, captivated by
grace which it senses lurking everywhere, does not easily give up
on the salvation of anyone. We weep for Mozart and for Violetta
and for Margarita, but we also suspect that, because grace is

everywhere, we will meet them all again. And perhaps Faust, too, and even the Don, because God's forgiving love has no limits.

If you doubt that a distinctive Catholic imagination animates these two operas, try comparing them to Benjamin Britten's *Peter Grimes*, a story of a man destroyed by the rigidities of his local community. There is no salvation for anyone at the end of the opera, no hint of hope. In *Peter Grimes*, the classic Protestant image of the individual fighting against an oppressive society—a paradigm which affects much of American elite culture—dominates. In the two Catholic operas, the individuals are supported by an imperfect but loving society.

In yet another story about the ubiquity and implacability of God's saving grace, the protagonist is cheerfully consigned to hell by members of her own congregation until God has His say. Lars von Trier's Cannes-prize-winning *Breaking the Waves* pushes the envelope of Catholic sensibility to its outrageous and graceful limit.

Bess (the luminous Emily Watson) is a simple, intensely loving young woman who lives among dour folk on an island off the coast of Scotland. Her family belongs to a Calvinist congregation so suspicious of sacraments that it has removed bells from the bell tower of its church. Bess, who talks to God in church and listens to His responses in a deeper version of her own voice, is thought to be devout but a little weak in the head. She falls in love with Jan, a Norwegian who works on an oil rig off the coast. In her marriage she finds powerful pleasure in sexual love, for which she thanks God, who seems, in a grudging Calvinist way, to approve of their passion (as well He should, since He created them with it!). Then Jan is paralyzed, presumably for life, in an accident for which Bess blames herself, since she had pleaded

Emily Watson in a scene from Lars von Trier's *Breaking the Waves*.

with God to send Jan home from the rig. Figuring, not unreasonably, that he is finished and knowing how much sex has come to mean to Bess, he urges her to find a lover. She feels she must do so to heal him. As his drug-fogged mind becomes more confused and she misunderstands (maybe) what God wants of her, she engages in random couplings, and then turns to prostitution on ships offshore. Jan seems to improve slightly, though no one around him notices it. Bess is expelled from her church, shunned, and stoned by the children of the parish.[1] God, who has been absent for a while, speaks to her again, now a gentle and loving God who assures her that He will always be with her, no matter what. She goes out to a ship which all the local prostitutes avoid because of the brutality of the crew and is violated and murdered.

At the coroner's inquest, the young doctor who had taken care of both Bess and Jan says that she died of goodness, which makes no sense to the coroner but a lot of sense to us, who have been privy to her perhaps mistaken but good intentions. Her congregation decides that there will be no service for her in church but that she will be buried in the cemetery (in a ceremony attended only by men!). The elders consign her to hell for her sinfulness. So, it would seem, ends the story of Bess, and this melancholy film with it. All right, the viewer says, Bess is a kind of Christ figure, laying down her life for someone she loves. But what else is von Trier trying to say?

Now Jan, ambulatory and recovering rapidly, along with his friends from the oil rig, steals her body and takes it out to sea for burial. Bells begin to peal, though, as the radio man on the rig says, there's nothing within five hundred miles that can be producing the sound. The bells ring and ring and ring as the film truly ends. God has rendered his verdict on Bess, vindicating her just as He vindicated Jesus, for whom she has become a metaphor, a sacrament. As the critic Roger Ebert observed, the film says that God not only knows everything but also understands more than most people give Him credit for.

The end of the film turns melancholy into triumph for Bess and Jan and, of course, God.[2] *Breaking the Waves*, for all its cinema verité technique and realism of setting, is in fact a fable, a parable, of grace superabundant, of a loving God who stands by us always, just as he promised Bess He would do.

Can there be any doubt that this film, despite its ostensibly Calvinist setting, is the result of a distinctive Catholic imagination? Compare Bess with Hardy's Tess of the d'Urbervilles, who dies without mercy or the hope of mercy—and destroyed by an oppressive community.

David Lodge's novels are hard to summarize because his ironic wit defies summary. His protagonists are often swept up by some kind of salvation—an imperfect and problematic salvation perhaps, but one in which there are not only grounds for hope but also powerful hints of grace. In *Paradise News*, Bernard Walsh is a priest-turned-atheist and university instructor whose dying aunt in Hawaii summons Bernard and his contentious father from England to her bedside. Off they go on a package tour filled with the usual tourist characters, affording Lodge a lot of fun with Oahu resorts. Then Bernard's father is hit by a car and bounced into a hospital (not seriously injured), where Bernard falls in love with Yolande, the woman who was driving the car. And she with him: she skillfully introduces him to the art of physical love. Relationships among the various characters are

stretched to the breaking point. Then his father and aunt reconcile, his sister and her husband reconcile, and a teenage woman
finds the courage to begin to defy her authoritarian father.
Bernard goes home to his classroom.

Near the end, in a lecture which is a caricature of atheistic
theology, complete with a misquote of the Catholic theologian
Karl Rahner, he shocks some of the nuns in his class by his rejection of life after death. Shortly thereafter, he receives a letter
from Yolande describing his aunt's funeral (a Mass on the beach
with hula dancers) and recounting the moving words of the
priest. When it becomes clear that Yolande, a skeptic, has begun
to believe in purpose (in grace, though she doesn't use the word),
the contrast between her intense new faith and his clichéd old
unbelief is lost on him but not on the reader, who smiles again at
Lodge's irony.

Yolande loves Bernard and will come to visit him at Christmas.
Shaken but happy, he sits on a bench in front of his school. A colleague asks him whether the letter contains "good news or bad."

"Oh, good," says Bernard. "Very good news."

The story, then, is not about paradise lost or paradise found
but about paradise news, which is very good news. Gospel.
Bernard has learned that he is loved and he has given love.
Grace. And new life, *metanoia*, a transforming change, bestowed
almost wantonly on many characters, as many as Lodge can possibly grant it to. As with Bess, God is drawing straight with
crooked lines in *Paradise News*, an abundance of crooked lines,
but God's graceful schemes are implacable. Moreover, God's
schemes are also "comic" in the classical sense of the word: serious events (a car accident, loss of faith) yield humorous results

(a love affair with one's father's assailant, conversion by a skeptic) and lead ultimately to happy endings.

Catholic artists and writers tend to hunger for the salvation of their characters—Greene's whiskey priest, Roddy Doyle's father in his Barrytown trilogy (played perfectly by Colm Meany in the film versions), Gounod's Margarita, Verdi's Violetta, Father Hugh in *The Edge of Sadness*, Bess in *Breaking the Waves*, Lodge's pilgrim in *Therapy*, or his former priest in *Paradise News*. They want salvation for the characters (and of course for themselves, too) because they find themselves in a grace-filled world, a world in which grace surges all around. A God who discloses Herself so recklessly, so prodigally, must necessarily be a God who wants salvation for all Her children. The Catholic sensibility, realistic indeed about the sufferings of life and the inevitability of death, is nonetheless at worst bittersweet (like the slow movement of Mozart's no. 26) but never, never desperate, never pessimistic, never hopeless. Sometimes the Catholic sensibility verges on stoicism, but even then it does not lose its capability to smile and even laugh. Catholic stoicism, like Catholicism, is distinctive.

The sensibility reflected by Mozart, Verdi, Gounod, von Trier, and Lodge is also present in ordinary Catholics. They tend to picture God, creation, the world, society, and themselves the way their great artists do—as drenched with grace, that is to say, with God's passionately forgiving love, His salvation.

Do ordinary Catholics, then, feel that the world is a place enchanted with abundant opportunities for salvation? Empirical measures (though not as precise as one might wish) can be found in items asked in several General Social Survey questionnaires in the 1980s. Respondents were asked to choose between seven pairs of descriptions of the "world":

1. The world is basically filled with sin and evil. . . . There is much goodness in the world which hints at God's goodness.

2. The good person must be deeply involved in the problems of the world. . . . The good person must avoid contamination by the corruption of the world.

3. God is almost totally removed from the sinfulness of the world. . . . God reveals Himself in and through the world.

4. Human nature is basically good. . . . Human nature is fundamentally perverse and corrupt.

5. Through such things as art and music we learn about God. . . . It is dangerous for humans to be too concerned about worldly things like art and music.

6. The world is a place of strife and disorder. . . . Harmony and cooperation prevail in the world.

7. Human achievement helps reveal God in the world. . . . Most human activity is vain and foolish.

On all but item 3, Catholics are significantly more likely than Protestants to endorse the more benign view of the world. By a margin of 68 percent to 56 percent, Catholics are more likely to feel that the world is good rather than evil; at 60 percent to 50 percent, they are more likely to think that a good person must be involved in the problems of the world; at 74 percent to 66 percent, they tend to believe that art and music teach about God. Catholics are more likely than Protestants to see God present in His creation and that creation as revealing Him. Creation is, to the Catholic sensibility, enchanting because it discloses the Enchanter.

As I said at the beginning of the book, Catholics live in God-haunted houses and an enchanted world. In a world where grace is everywhere, the haunting and enchanting go on constantly. Clearly, the world of the great Catholic artists and writers is enchanted. The thesis of the present essay is that they see reality the way they do *because* they either grew up Catholic or were attracted to Catholicism as adults by virtue of its enchanting aspects. They reflect an enchantment that permeates the Catholic community, a haunting that hints powerfully at a salvation guaranteed by pervasive grace.

That sort of enchantment may not be the goal of becoming a mature Catholic adult, but it certainly is an excellent place to begin.

The bells of the Kölner Dom peal in celebration of the Catholic stories treasured in that astonishing church. The bells of Bess's church (which no longer exist!) peal to celebrate her vindication by God. In such a world of pealing bells, there can be only enchantment.

And salvation!

CHAPTER SEVEN

Sensibility and Socialization

The conventional wisdom of pop sociology is that everyone is becoming more like everyone else. The mass media, the jet airplane, the Internet are homogenizing humankind (or, at least, American humankind) at a rapid rate. Differences among humans are disappearing, and that is probably a good thing. If, therefore, there remains a Catholic religious sensibility, it is declining. Catholics are rapidly becoming like everyone else.

There is no evidence to support such generalizations—no correlation, for instance, between youth and more advanced education (factors presumed to enhance this homogenization) on the one hand and lower scores on the measures of a distinctive Catholic religious sensibility on the other. Yet the question remains whether such a religious imagination can survive when church leaders and theologians ignore it and the new generation of Catholic thinkers seems resolutely unaware of it.

OPPOSITE: Nuns escort a group of girls, dressed for their First Communion, across a street in Puerto Rico. Courtesy CORBIS.

The answer is that religious sensibilities do not depend on scholars or bureaucrats for continuity. They are passed on locally, intimately, without any particular regard for what may be going on in the high tradition. The transmission of the Catholic sexual sensibility I described in Chapter 2 is but a specific example of a more general phenomenon.

If the reader, despite profound skepticism about whether there is a Catholic imagination which differs at least partly from the Protestant imagination, is willing to concede, based on the empirical evidence, that Catholics view reality somewhat differently, the question then arises as to how this comes to be. How is it that Catholics live in a world that is enchanted, despite the fact that their church leaders and thinkers are incorrigibly prosaic and seem to have hardened their hearts against the poetry of religion? Granted, for the sake of argument, that Catholics are more interested in the fine arts, more experimental in their sexual behavior, more sympathetic to women and AIDS victims, more community oriented, more concerned about social justice, more aware of the necessity of social structure and hence more involved in social concerns, and more aware of the presence of saving grace, how do they come to be that way? Granted also that the worldview of Catholic artists and writers reflects the religious sensibility of Catholic people, how did the laity get that worldview in the first place, especially since the dull prosody of their theologians and bishops and most of their clergy and educators is utterly innocent of any sense of enchantment? How does one acquire a Catholic sensibility, a Catholic perspective on time and space and community and creation and salvation?

The answer is that a religious sensibility is passed on by story-tellers, most of whom are not aware that they are telling stories because their narratives reside more in who they are and what they do rather than in what they say. Religious heritages are transmitted, not necessarily by official teachers and preachers, but more likely by intimates, those who are closest to us in our lives. The stories are told by the way in which they react to the ordinary and especially the extraordinary events of life—failure, disappointment, suffering, injustice, death, success, joy, love, intense pleasure, marriage, birth.

In our study of young Catholics, my colleagues and I tried to confirm this answer to the question of where the Catholic sensibility comes from, which is in fact the same as the more general question of how all religious heritages are transmitted across generational lines. Using detailed analysis that need not be rehearsed here, our Study of Young Catholics found that the Catholic sensibility is passed on first through the stories one hears at the dawn of consciousness and that slip, via images and pictures (the Madonna, the crèche), subtly into that consciousness during the early years of life. Then through the various socializing influences in the young person's life—parents, siblings, relatives, teachers, friends, the parish community, the spouse, the liturgy, and religious and even theological reading. The playing field is tilted in favor of the Catholic sensibility from the beginning of consciousness and remains tilted—not perfectly, not necessarily permanently, more strongly in some than in others, but tilted nonetheless.

The strongest religious socializing influences are, not surprisingly, parents, religious experience, closeness to nature, friends, religious community, quality of religious education, quality of preaching, and spouse, each adding a new layer of religious influence to previous layers. Of these, the most powerful are the parents and spouse. A spouse of several years who is a fulfilling sexual partner is the ultimate and most powerful of socializing influences. The individual religious sensibilities of such spouses tend to merge in a joint narrative, a joint religious sensibility.

Another analysis of the Young Catholics study data shows how conflicting religious narratives, one from the past and the other from the present, might work themselves out. Those young Catholic women who in the late 1970s thought that a child would not suffer if the mother worked and that women should be ordained priests were 17 percentage points less likely to attend church services regularly than those who did not hold both of those positions. Four influences seem to account for the differences. The "angry" feminists, as opposed to those who were feminist but went to church regularly, tended to be nonworking wives who were dissatisfied with their family situation, whose mothers were devout, and whose mothers had not worked when their own children were small. Apparently, their mothers had communicated to these young women an image of the appropriate role of women which was incompatible with the young women's feminist principles. However, this conflict between mother's model and daughter's model was canceled out if five new circumstances were at work: the husband went to church regularly, the husband also was a feminist, the marriage was sexually satisfying, the husband was judged by the wife to be religiously influential, and God was pictured as a lover. In turn, the picture of God as a lover was enhanced by two events outside the

A religious service in the church of the Holy Family Parish in Chicago. Courtesy Franklin McMahon, CORBIS.

family context: judgment that priests in the parish were sympathetic and a report that the woman had had a serious discussion with a priest recently.

Let us suppose an imaginary case to tie these data together. A feminist who has drifted away from the Church had acquired in her early socialization experience the Catholic narrative, but in a context which specified a highly constrained role for women. Her religious sensibility was sharply challenged by the feminist ideology which she acquired in later socialization experiences. The woman's preference was now to move away from a heritage which she perceived as imposing her mother's ideology. However, she encountered other socializing agents, either a sympathetic priest or a satisfactory husband or both, who provided an opposing narrative which tilted her back in the direction of her original heritage so that she renewed her repertory of stories with a more sophisticated interpretation concerning the role of women.

The woman's encounter with agents of the feminist story created a crisis in her continued acceptance of prior religious socialization. The agents told an appealing story of equality for women which questioned her received narrative of constrained womanhood and told her that she threatened her own social capital if she adhered to the old stories. Subsequently, she encountered other new socialization agents who retold—perhaps more in attitude than in words—the original narrative so that it was no longer incompatible with what had become her ideological preference. Thus, she was able to return to her earlier sensibility with a more nuanced understanding of it.

A certain kind of Catholic, sometimes writing for the conservative journal *Crisis* and sometimes for the liberal journal *The*

Commonweal (which now sometimes claims to be moderate), complains about the declining faith of Catholic children. The Church, they argue, is no longer doing an adequate job of educating them and Catholicism as a result is patently in decline. Somehow, they seem pleased to be heralds of this bad news. Rarely does it occur to these writers that the primary religious educational responsibility is theirs, not the Church's. Formal Catholic education makes an important contribution but cannot substitute for family influence. Moreover, I can find no evidence in the empirical data to confirm their fears, which suggest rather that a religious sensibility has extraordinary durability. It has lasted fifteen hundred years, plus or minus a couple of centuries. It is unlikely to disappear.

Where, then, does the institutional Church fit into the paradigm I have been describing? Parents, relatives, neighbors, friends, teachers, classmates, local clergy, lovers, and above all spouses are the primary religious socializers, the most powerful sources of the Catholic sensibility. The papacy and the hierarchy are usually mediated through these local socialization agents, or through a thirty-second clip on the evening news or a seven-hundred-fifty-word press association dispatch. The typical Catholic probably has never read a papal or hierarchical document or listened with any attention to what a pope or a bishop has said. They probably have sat through religious instruction in Catholic school and may even have read a book or two beyond the textbook. But these are weak influences compared to stories told by the family, the peer group, the parish priest, and the spouse.

Theologians are an even weaker influence. Most Catholics have never heard of them. If they have heard of them, they do not read them. If they do read them, they don't know what they are talking about.

Thus, even well-educated and sophisticated Catholics have acquired their Catholic sensibility almost entirely through stories told by local socialization agents. The mistake of many Catholic leaders is to assume that what they say and do really matters or has ever mattered *unless local socialization agents are willing to tell the same stories.* Who has more influence on religious preference, the pope or a warmly loving spouse? If you are not sure of the answer to that question, then you are kidding yourself.

Attempts by the high tradition to change this local Catholicism have never been very successful and are not likely ever to be so, unless the leadership is willing to listen to what the men and women, the laity and clergy in the local places are trying to say, unless the leadership gives up its propensity to answer questions no one is asking and ignore the questions everyone is asking. Leadership will have impact on the popular tradition only when it becomes adept enough to be able to speak from within that tradition instead of outside it, only when the leaders too are open to enchantment.

The Enchanted Imagination

I f a reader were of a mind to, it would be easy to pick this essay apart on the grounds that the correlation between the vision of Catholic art and the imagination of ordinary Catholics is not proved conclusively. Such a reader could also assert that there are many different kinds of Catholic imagination, some of them strikingly different.

Such responses, I submit, miss the point entirely. The present essay is not a definitive statement about either the Catholic artistic sensibility or the Catholic popular sensibility, nor is it about the similarities between them or how they might influence one another. It is at most a preliminary inquiry into a remarkably suggestive coincidence, one which deserves careful consideration. If the coincidence points to an underlying dynamism that flourishes within the Catholic community and has flourished there for centuries, then that dynamism almost demands detailed exploration. I have attempted little more than to raise the question.

OPPOSITE: A sand rendition of the Pieta on the beach at Ocean City, Maryland. Photo by Paul A. Souders, courtesy CORBIS.

"You're biased in favor of Catholicism," a European monk wrote to me after he had read the first draft of this essay.

Well, yes. I'm a Catholic. I like being a Catholic. I did not write this essay to attack Catholicism. Rather, I have tried to explain what I think the Catholic imagination is, namely, one that views the world and all that is in it as enchanted, haunted by the Holy Spirit and the presence of grace. If that religious sensibility is, in its best moments, attractive, then it is not my fault and not the result of my attempts to manipulate the data to make Catholicism look good. I could also write a book listing all the things which are wrong with Catholicism in its present institutional manifestations. Indeed, I have written such books.

My goal has been modest. I merely wish to show that there is a low-level correlation between the great works of art created by Catholics and the imaginations of ordinary Catholics, that there is a correlation between the sensibility of Nicholas of Verdun, Bernini, St. John of the Cross, Hopkins, Greene, Scorsese, Vermeer, and Mozart on the one hand and ordinary Catholic laity today on the other. There can be no question that those worthies were Catholic. Moreover, the empirical data which I cite to suggest such a correlation is on the public record and can be analyzed by anyone. I did not make up the findings that Catholics are more concerned about community and social issues and enjoy sex more.

I don't want to argue with anyone who is not Catholic. I certainly do not want to suggest that Catholicism is better than your religion, only that it seems to be different. Again, I have shown only that the null hypothesis that there is a distinctive Catholic imagination cannot be rejected—a modest enough claim.

We saw in the previous chapter that the confusion of the years since the Second Vatican Council has not weakened the Catholic sensibility among younger Catholics. A study conducted at the Catholic University of America of a representative sample of young Catholics reports that the four strongest indicators of Catholic identity among younger Catholics are concern for the poor, the presence of God in the sacraments, the real presence in the Eucharist, and devotion to Mary. While *The Commonweal*—which reported the findings in its July 17, 1998, issue—thought that these factors were evidence of a "faith loosely held" (their title) and a decline from some unspecified level of faith held in the past, it seems to me that they are in fact evidence of a sensibility irrevocably held. The enchanted imagination is alive and well among these young people. Sacrament, community, and Mary—what more could one ask for?

Suppose that you, gentle reader, are a Catholic. Having considered the enchantment touched upon in this essay, perhaps some of you will understand a little more clearly why you hang on to your heritage, despite the problems you may have with some of your leaders. Perhaps others of you who are bitterly angry at Catholicism will pause to ponder what is good about it, a goodness that human frailty and malice cannot destroy.

And those of you who are leaders and teachers—of whatever ideological hue—may ponder the possibility that you might have missed completely a powerful and critically important component of the Catholic heritage, that indeed you might be prosaic persons surrounded by enchantment. At a minimum, you might admit that enchantment is more important than you thought it was, whether the enchantment of St. Xavier del Bac or Hopkins's

"May Magnificat," of a First Communion or a May crowning or a burning votive candle, of a church that looks like a church instead of a—heaven save us all—worship center. Those of you who insist that, because most Catholics now deny the right of their religious leaders to control their sexual lives, they are no different from Protestants, might want to ponder the question of whether there is more to the Catholic heritage than sex and authority. In the most important matter, the uniquely Catholic views of God, their world, and the relationship between the two continue to be durable—unchanged and probably unchangeable.

Now suppose that you are not Catholic. You might want to consider the possibility that you have misunderstood Catholicism. What you have always dismissed as weird mumbo jumbo combined with pathetic stubbornness may be utterly consistent with an implicit but systematic way of looking at reality. It may not be your way of looking at reality. You might not want to imagine a world in which God lurks everywhere and people respond to Him as a community. Fair enough. I won't try to talk you out of that position. But at least you should be willing to admit that it is a legitimate way of imagining reality and to respect the consistency with which Catholic behavior fits that imagination.

Imagine, if you will, my separated brother or sister, that you see a large crowd of Catholics wildly cheering a pope, any pope. You could marvel at the intellectual weakness of such subservience to the teachings of a man who is human like the rest of us. Or you could be shocked by the hypocrisy of people who cheer for their leader while ignoring his injunctions in their everyday sex life.

A multitude of saints in the sanctuary at San Xavier del Bac Mission.

I suggest to you that you consider the possibility that the crowd of Catholics is cheering for itself, for its Church, and for its unity in diversity. The pope symbolizes the Church and God's presence in it. It is not a perfect Church and he is not a perfect man. He makes mistakes under ordinary circumstances, just as the rest of us do. The cheering Catholics who may disagree vehemently with the pope on many issues—and he would tell them that they are wrong to do so—nonetheless applaud him not out of mindless obedience but because of enthusiasm for a way of looking at life which they learned from their intimate and local relationships. The pope confirms for them that the enchantment is real, that grace is everywhere, that the stories they've heard are true.

Grand Beach
JUNE 1997

Tucson
MARCH 1998

Grand Beach
AUGUST 1998

A NOTE ON SOURCES

All the data cited in this book are based on representative national sample surveys, especially the General Social Survey, an annual survey conducted for the National Science Foundation by the National Opinion Research Center (NORC) since 1972. Generally, there are approximately fifteen hundred respondents in each survey. My data on Catholic sexual imagery and on the Catholic liturgical imagination are based on the GSS. The GSS data set is available from the Roper Institute.

International data are taken from the International Survey Program archived at the Central Archives (ZA) of the University of Köln and from the European Value Study archived at the University of Sussex in England. The minimum size of an ISP data file for a given country is one thousand respondents.

Data on priests are based on the 1970 study of the Catholic priesthood conducted by NORC for the Catholic bishops. Data on young Catholics are based on the 1979 study of young Catholics conducted by NORC for the Knights of Columbus.

Data sets are available from NORC (1155 East 60 Street, Chicago, IL 60637).

More recent data on priests are based on a survey conducted by the *Los Angeles Times;* see "Catholics Favor Married and Female Priests, Survey Finds," June 1, 1996. Data on sexual behavior are also based on a survey conducted by Gallup for *Psychology Today.*

Finally, readers may find useful the discussion of "The Ecstasy of St. Teresa" on pp. 26 and 90–93 of Scribner, *Bernini* (New York: Abrams, 1991); Anthony S. Bryk, with Valerie Lee and Peter Holland, *Catholic Schools in the Common Good* (Cambridge: Harvard University Press, 1993); Jeff Manza and Clem Brooks, "The Religious Factor in U.S. Presidential Elections 1960–1992," *AJS* 103 (July 1997): 38–81; Michael Schuck, "The Content and Coherence of Roman Catholic Encyclical Social Teaching: 1740–1987," Ph.D. thesis, University of Chicago Divinity School, June 1988; or several other of my own works: *Priests in the U.S.: Reflections on a Survey* (New York: Doubleday, 1972); with Joan Fee, William C. McCready, and Teresa Sullivan, *Young Catholics in the United States and Canada* (New York: William H. Sadlier, Inc., 1981); *The Religious Imagination* (New York: Sadlier, 1981); *Faithful Attraction: Discovering Intimacy, Love, and Fidelity in American Marriage* (New York: Tor Books, 1991); and "Pie in the Sky While You're Still Alive," a paper presented at the meeting of the American Sociological Association, 1996.

NOTES

INTRODUCTION
The Sacraments of Sensibility

1. Research that my colleague Wolfgang Jagodzinski has done shows that superstition is still commonplace in European countries, though surprisingly less prevalent in countries where either faith or atheism is strong (Ireland and East Germany, respectively) and more prevalent in countries where both faith and atheism are weak (Britain and West Germany). Jagodzinski, "Superstition in Contemporary Europe," unpublished paper, 1996.

2. As I have argued in my book *Religion as Poetry* (New Brunswick: Transaction Press, 1995).

3. There is a certain form of Catholic political correctness which will surely complain that I pay no attention in this essay to the third world. Stories told in Africa or Latin America, some will say, are not the same stories that can be told in the West. Although that is doubtless the case, it is also evident that the structures of myths are similar (albeit, as Wendy Doniger has observed, flesh and bones are far more interesting than skeletons). As a professional storyteller, I am well

aware that the same story can be told over and over again in many different forms.

4. David Tracy, *The Analogical Imagination* (New York: Crossroads, 1982).

5. Perhaps all metaphors are also implicit narratives, but that argument need not detain us.

6. Bede, *Ecclesiastical History I*, xxx, trans. Colgrave, *Bede's Ecclesiastical History*, pp. 106–109.

7. In a certain sense, the most difficult conflict within Catholicism is between this instinct that nature is revelatory and the Platonism of St. Augustine, who distrusted and feared nature. The former appears to be winning at long last, but only an unwise gambler would bet on its final victory any time soon. Orthodoxy, which has never liked Augustine all that much, has avoided this conflict.

8. In many of the databases on which I will rely, there are not enough Protestant respondents to break them into separate denominations. When it is possible to distinguish denominational heritages I will do so. In general, members of liberal Protestant denominations (Anglicans, Presbyterians, Methodists) are much more like Catholics than are more moderate and conservative Protestants. The differences among Protestant imaginations is a fascinating subject, but one beyond the scope of this essay.

CHAPTER ONE
Sacred Place, Sacred Time

1. In excavations several layers beneath the present Dom, there is a room which was once part of the large (heated) Roman house which was the first of Köln's churches.

2. Repairs are continuous. When the Dom is finished, say the Kölners with a wink, it will be the end of the world.

3. There are three Irish pubs in Köln. Heinrich Böll, the Nobel laureate novelist, was married to an Irish woman and wrote a wonderfully

perceptive book about Ireland. Moreover, the political and business styles of the city, shaped by informal networks and patronage (called "Kölnsch Klungel"), are not unlike those of Ireland. Or of Chicago, for that matter.

4. "Kölner" is the more formal adjective. "Kölnsch" is a word from the local dialect and is never used of the Dom.

5. Eileen Kane has written a brilliant essay comparing the opinions of two thirteenth-century French abbots on the subject of the beauty of church buildings—St. Bernard of Clairveaux and Suger of Saint-Denis. The former argued for economy and simplicity, the latter for elaborate—and expensive—beauty. Both were right: there is room in the Catholic sensibility for both.

6. David Tracy, noting that there were no great theologians in the era of the Counter-Reformation, has argued that baroque art, architecture, and music were the "classics" of the Catholic tradition for that time. I am not an enthusiastic admirer of baroque churches (though I revel in baroque music); indeed, I tell Jesuit friends that all Jesuit churches (like the Martinkirche in Bamberg and Jesuitenkirche in Mannheim) look alike—great barns covered with gilt.

7. Teresa's parents argue in the death room about the garden. The mother (Tracey Ullman) insists that the father (Vincent D'Onofrio) only imagined that the garden was not in bloom the day before. I couldn't remember what the garden looked like, but when I reversed the tape I discovered that the Ms. Savoca was definitely on the father's side.

8. A national probability sample of Americans, who were surveyed in personal interviews. The analysis on which this essay is based included 1,365 Americans who identified as either Catholic or Protestant. In a sample this size, there are not enough respondents from other religious backgrounds for analysis—only twenty-nine Jews, for example. Moreover, with the exception of the Baptists, there are not enough from individual Protestant denominations to make comparisons between them and Catholics possible. NORC has developed a category which

enables one to divide Protestants into fundamentalist, moderate, and liberal. In the analysis on which this essay is based, comparisons were made between Catholics and fundamentalist Protestants, and Catholics and a combination of moderate and liberal Protestants. While the second group of Protestants was more likely to be involved with the fine arts than the former, these two comparisons did not differ substantially from the comparison with all Protestants reported in the present essay.

9. The data from the General Social Survey are available at almost every university computer center in the country; see A Note on Sources.

10. More precisely, in the logic of social science, the null hypothesis that this model did not acceptably fit the data had to be rejected.

11. And who could be more "dialectical" than Søren Kirkegaard? And what more "analogical" than a pilgrimage to Santiago de Campostela?

CHAPTER TWO
Sacred Desire

1. This analysis is based in part on research reported in my book *Sex: The Catholic Experience* (Chicago: Thomas More Press, 1995).

2. From *The Collected Works of St. John of the Cross*, trans. Kieran Kavanaugh and Otilio Rodriguez (Washington, D.C.: ICS Publications, 1979). Courtesy the Institute of Carmelite Studies.

3. Leo Steinberg, *The Sexuality of Christ in Renaissance Art and in Modern Oblivion* (New York: Pantheon, 1982).

4. Even today there is a strain of Catholic ideology which denies that Jesus was fully human in all things, sin alone excepted. A parish at which I worked immediately after the Second Vatican Council was investigated by the Chicago chancery on Roman orders for preaching heresy. It turned out that the offensive phrase was taken from the Easter Gospel in which the angel says to those at the tomb, "You seek the Man Jesus, he is not here...." The translation was that approved by the American bishops. The representative from the chancery, instead of

reprimanding the complainant, warned us that we had to be careful about scandalizing the laity.

5. Some of which have been removed in current restorations of the *Last Judgment*—though not all of them yet.

CHAPTER THREE
The Mother Love of God

1. The research in this chapter was originally reported in my book *Young Catholics*.

2. Some Catholic feminists say that the Holy Spirit ought to represent the maternal or feminine dimension of God. Their argument is an example of the either/or approach to metaphors taken by those who have lost all sense of the fundamentally poetic dimension of religion.

3. These findings are described in greater detail in my book *The Religious Imagination*.

CHAPTER FOUR
Community

1. Brian DePalma's films are an exception, but the exception that fits the rule: DePalma is not Catholic.

2. Lee Lourdeaux, Italian and Irish Filmmakers in America (Philadelphia: Temple University Press, 1990).

3. There were and are successful Irish filmmakers. Lourdeaux writes persuasively about John Ford's Irish sensibility. However, it is more than just a stereotype to say that the Italian tradition is particularly good with visual metaphors and the Irish with verbal ones.

4. With all due respect to *the* University, splendid place that it is, I have learned that it does not lack for limitations of its own. Farrell never really realized this fact, or at least the characters in his stories never did.

5. Who was also based on one of Sister Liguori's classmates. I asked Sister once whether the woman knew about the book and knew that she was Lucy. "I never had the nerve to ask her," she replied. "But I think she did."

6. He was dead before I began to write my own stories, but out of tribute to him one of my families is also named Ryan.

7. Reanalysis of Weber's data indicates that he was mistaken. Certainly, Catholics do not lag in achievement measures in either America or today's Germany.

8. From the viewpoint of both capitalists and socialists. However, it was not unlike the worldview of nineteenth-century European anarchists like Pierre-Joseph Proudhon.

9. Many would-be Catholic intellectuals like to report the decline of the neighborhood and parish and to raise the question of whether the parish is the best way to minister to people. But this is dinner party talk and is not based on any evidence that parishes are declining or that most American Catholics are discontent with the parish as an institution, if not their own parish.

10. The countries were Great Britain, the United States, the Netherlands, Australia, and Hungary.

11. I leave out Catholic Poles because Poland joined the International Social Survey Program only recently. I omit Hispanics because Spain is also a recent addition and it is not clear to me that such a comparison would be appropriate, given that most Spanish-speaking Americans come from countries in the Americas.

12. All the differences reported in this and subsequent paragraphs in this chapter are statistically significant.

13. Britain, Canada, the United States, Australia, and Ireland (all thirty-two counties).

14. James S. Coleman, with Thomas Hoffer and Sally Kilgore, *High School Achievement: Public, Catholic, and Private Schools Compared* (New York: Basic Books, 1982).

15. Including the white disadvantaged student.

CHAPTER FIVE
Hierarchy

1. Everyone is entitled to his own reading of *Finnegans Wake*. Berry Schlossman sees it as being structured around the Tenebrae services which marked the culmination of Holy Week before the Second Vatican Council. Without denying Ms. Schlossman's reading, I see the novel as an exercise in which Joyce, among many other things, imagines what his life might have been like if he and Nora had not fled Dublin. Whatever the reading, the story is framed at beginning and end by the Liffey River which flows through the middle of Dublin and organizes the city.

2. Kells was an Irish monastery.

3. It was, however, a Catholic, Lord Acton, who described what others call the "iron law of oligarchy" as "Power corrupts, absolute power corrupts absolutely." Ironically, he was referring to the Vatican. There is surely a tendency for power to corrupt, and that tendency must be resisted by some sort of system of checks and balances.

4. However, despite the insistence on the literal inerrancy of the Bible by the Southern Baptist Convention, only 57 percent of Southern Baptists accept this teaching, as do less than half of the churchgoing Southern Baptists under forty years old. Catholics, it seems, have no monopoly on dissent from religious authority.

5. A principle which has been formulated under that term by the European Union with appropriate reference to Pope Pius XI, who coined it in 1929.

6. Strangely enough, Ireland, although it claims to be founded on Catholic principles, has one of the most centralized political structures in Europe. The men who framed its constitution apparently had not read either the encyclicals or James Joyce.

7. Close feeling toward one's county, or a lack thereof, is perhaps not indicative of much in the United States, but it is perhaps significant in the British isles.

8. He reminds me of his present successor in the See of St. Ambrose, Cardinal Carlo Maria Martini, one of the great churchmen of our era, who is also wise and learned and holy, as well as witty (a trait which Manzoni did not report of Cardinal Borromeo).

9. O'Brien and Crosby, they say, lacked liturgical awareness and social concern. These critics seem to forget that there are many generous and happy priests like those portrayed in the films of the two actors. The portraits may lack complexity, but they are not fundamentally inaccurate.

10. As film critic Roger Ebert pointed out in his newspaper column at the time of the film's premiere.

11. In my role as someone who tells stories about priests—almost all of whom, like the ineffable Blackie Ryan, would be in the upper percentile of priests on a scale of admirability—I have found that one is attacked by both sides. The integralist reactionaries denounce me for the sin of not presenting "edifying" priests—Blackie drinks too much, though he's never drunk—while left-wing feminists assail me because my priests are not all perfect models in their relationships with women. Such critics share the false assumption that stories are for education and indoctrination and not for illumination.

12. Played by Gerard Depardieu in the Cannes-prize-winning film based on the novel.

CHAPTER SIX
Salvation

1. The film critic for the National Catholic Reporter attacked *Breaking the Waves* on ideological grounds. Those who thought it was a "woman's film," he wrote, were wrong: it was a "man's film," indeed, a male chauvinist film. Thus do ideologues miss the point and the presence of grace.

2. While watching the film, I was offended by the hypocrisy of the clergyman and the elders of the Calvinist congregation. Then I realized that Catholicism is not without similarly arrogant people, some of them among the power elites in the Vatican.

INDEX

abortion, attitudes toward, 105, 131

absence of God, from the world, 5, 17

Acton, Lord John, 197n3

Adams, Henry, 99

Adenauer, Konrad, 25–26

AIDS, 144, 174

Albert the Great, 25

allegory, Song of Songs seen as, 61

Alone of All Her Sex (Warner), 105

analogical imagination, 50, 194n11. *See also* imagination, Catholic

Analogical Imagination (Tracy), 5–7

analogy, relationship to metaphor, 7–8

Anderson, Sherwood, 117

Angles, the, missionaries to, 11–12

Animal Farm (Orwell), 141

anthropomorphic language, predicated of God, 8–9

Apocalypse Now (film), 112

architecture, 3, 33, 37; Norman cathedrals, 94–95

Arian heresy, 71

Arizona, University of, 128–29

"Ash Wednesday" (Eliot), 99

atheism, relationship to superstition, 191n1

Augustine (of Hippo), St., 192n7; on sexual desire and sexual union, 60, 61–62, 75–76, 80–81, 82, 85–86

Augustine of Canterbury, St., Pope Gregory's message to, 11–12, 13, 15, 17, 36

Australia: European Values Study, 130–32, 196n13; International Social Survey Program research, 127–28, 196n10

authority, religious, dissent from, 142, 197n4

Authority in the Free Church Tradition (Harrison), 141–42

Baptists, 106, 197n4
baroque art, architecture, and music, 193n6; churches, 33, 37
Bathsheba at the Fountain (Rubens), 58 (fig.)
beauty, of sacred places, 33, 193n5
Belloc, Hilaire, 47–48
bells, 163, 165, 170
Benedictine abbeys, 33
Bernanos, Georges, 20; *Diary of a Country Priest*, 39, 78, 156; *Under the Son of Satan*, 39, 156, 198n12
Bernard of Clairvaux, St., 101, 193n5
Bernini, Giovanni, 75, 86, 184; sculpture of St. Theresa, 54 (fig.), 57, 63, 64 (fig.), 65
Bible, the. *See* Scripture(s)
birth control, attitudes toward, 105
bishops, 137–38
Böll, Heinrich, 192n3
Bomfim (Our Lord of the Happy Death), feast of, in Brazil, 14–15
Book of Common Prayer, Sarum rite marriage ritual, 61
Book of Kells, 18, 139, 197n2
Bottega di Tomaso di Vigilia, *Madonna and Child*, 88 (fig.)
Brazil, feast of Bomfim, 14–15
Breaking the Waves (film), 39, 163–66, 164 (fig.), 168, 170, 198nn1, 2
breast, female, eroticism of, 65
Brigid (goddess), 12
Britten, Benjamin, *Peter Grimes*, 163
Brody, Sister Liguori, 118, 196n5
Brooks, Clem, analysis of voting patterns, 144–45
Bryk, Anthony, 133–34
Buchanan, Pat, 144, 145

burial of Jesus, paintings of, emphasis on genital areas, 71
Byzantine art and architecture, 70, 72, 96

Calvinism, portrayal in *Breaking the Waves*, 163, 165–66, 198n2
Canada, European Values Study, 130–32, 196n13
Capra, Frank, *It's a Wonderful Life*, 112
Carroll, Michael, 20
cathedrals, 26, 33, 94–95. *See also* Köln, Cathedral
Catholic Legion of Decency, 149
Catholic Schools and the Common Good (Bryk et al.), 133–34
Catholic University of America, 185
celibacy for the clergy, support for, 155
Chartres Cathedral, 33, 95
Chaucer, Geoffrey, 61, 81, 152
Chicago, 193n3; Farrell's novels based in, 117–21; Holy Family Parish church, 177 (fig.)
Chicago, University of, 119, 195n4
Christ Carrying the Cross (Francesco de Maineri), 158 (fig.)
church attendance, Catholic, positive correlations: with fine arts consumption, 42–45, 50; with valuing of leisure, 52
church attendance, Protestant, negative correlations: with fine arts consumption, 42, 44; with valuing of leisure, 52
churches, 33–39; cathedrals, 26, 33, 94–95; in Köln, 23, 24–25, 192n1. *See also* Köln, Cathedral
Cignani, Carlo, 75; *Joseph and the Wife of Potiphar*, 66–67, 68 (fig.)

"Classmates of Studs, The"
(Brody), 118
clergy, Catholic, 147–48, 179;
concern over Mary metaphor,
99–100; hierarchy, 137–38;
laity's views of and relationships
with, 147–48, 154–57, 178; literary and film portrayals, 147,
149, 152–54, 155–56, 168,
198nn8–11 *(see also Diary of a
Country Priest; Power and the
Glory, The)*; in the Middle Ages,
13, 80
clergy, Protestant, laity's relationship to, 155
Coleman, James, 133–34
Commonweal, The (journal),
178–79, 185
community, 117, 123–33, 137,
174, 184, 196n9; and Catholic
approach to education, 133–35;
importance in Italian American
films, 112–13, 115, 117, 121;
image of measured against empirical data, 143–47; nature of
as ordered, 138, 141, 142–43;
portrayal in Farrell's novels,
117–21
conception of children (procreation), sexual pleasure for purpose of: in Augustinian and neo-
Platonic tradition, 60, 61–62; as
Catholic teaching, 75
Conrad, Joseph, *Heart of Darkness*, 112
conservatives, Catholics seen as,
144–46
continent, feeling toward one's,
143–44
Counter Reformation, 13, 40,
71–72, 193n6

county, feeling toward one's,
143–44; significance in the
British isles, 197n7
creation, 10; metaphorical nature
of, 5–6, 77
Crisis (journal), 178
Crosby, Bing, 154, 156, 198n9
crucifixion, paintings of, emphasis on genital areas of Jesus'
body, 71
"cultural" (lapsed) Catholics, 3
Cuomo, Mario, 112, 113–14
Cyril, St., 17

damnation. *See* salvation
Dante, 61; *The Divine Comedy*,
18, 81
Death of Nora Ryan, The (Farrell),
120–21
deities, female: Mary's function
similar to, 91, 94; maternal
image, 102
Delcambre, La., blessing of the
shrimping fleet, 136 (fig.)
Democratic voting patterns in
presidential elections, 145
demystification, 2–3
demythologization, 2–3
DeNiro, Robert, 111, 114 (fig.), 115
DePalma, Brian, 195n1
Depardieu, Gerard, 198n12
devotions, 5, 50, 78
dialectical imagination, 8, 50,
194n11
Diary of a Country Priest
(Bernanos), 39, 78, 156
dioceses, papal control of, 137–38
disadvantaged students, in Catholic high schools, 134, 196n15
Divine Comedy, The (Dante), 18, 81
divine love. *See* love of God

"Do Black Patent Leather Shoes Really Reflect Up?" (Powers), 100

doctrinal orthodoxy, on the Madonna Scale, 103–4

Dom, at Köln. *See* Köln, Cathedral

Don Giovanni (Mozart), 162–63

Doniger, Wendy, 191n3

Donovan, John, 123

Dublin, as setting for Joyce's *Ulysses*, 139–40

Dubus, Andre, 2

Duns Scotus, 25

Durkheim, Emile, 123

Easter, derivation of name for, 12

Easter Vigil, erotic imagery, 57

Eastren (goddess), 12

Ebert, Roger, 166, 198n10

ecstasy, divine: of St. Theresa, sculpture, 54 (fig.), 57, 64 (fig.). *See also* erotic desire

Ecstasy of St. Theresa (Bernini), 64 (fig.)

ecumenism: Mary doctrines played down in quest for, 101; reflected in church architecture, 34

Edge of Sadness (O'Connor), 121, 147, 168

education, 179; Catholic schools, 100, 101; high school achievement test scores, 133–35; inhibited by Catholic communalism for Weber, 123, 196n7

Eliot, T.S., "Ash Wednesday," 99

Ellis, Msgr. John Tracy, 123

enchantment, 1–3, 168–70, 174, 185, 187; missing in most theologians, clergy, and educators, 174, 180

erotic desire, 16, 55–57, 62, 65–66; as metaphor, 75; portrayal in art, 54 (fig.), 55, 57–70, 58 (fig.), 64 (fig.), 68–69 (figs.). *See also* imagery, sexual; sexual behavior/sexuality

ethical concerns, Catholic and Protestant attitudes compared, 130–33

ethos, Catholic, empirical indicators of, 127–32

Eucharist, the, 4, 33, 46, 78, 185

European Union, principle of subsidiarity, 197n5

European Values Study, 127, 130–32, 146, 196n13

faith: among young Catholics, *Commonweal*'s view of, 179, 185; apparent relationship of superstition to weakness of, 191n1; shaped by Catholic imagination, 31

Familiaris Consoritio (John Paul II), 79–80

family: importance in Italian American films, 112–13, 115; Irish American, portrayal in Farrell's *Studs Lonigan*, 118–19; ordering of power in, 141; relationships, Catholic and Protestant attitudes compared, 128–29, 131–32; role in transmitting Catholic sensibility, 175–76, 179. *See also* spouse(s)

Fanning, Charles, 119

Farrell, James T., 117–21, 126

father, versus mother, image of God as, 43

Faust (Gounod), 19, 162–63, 168

feasts. *See* festivals

feminism, 155, 176, 178, 198n11

feminists, Catholic: criticism of Mary metaphor and devotions, 100, 105; on the Holy Spirit as representing feminine dimension of God, 91

fertility cults, 94

festivals, 14–15, 47–52, 111; developed by parishioners of San Xavier Church, 38; efforts to strip from the liturgy, 50

films, 149, 151 (fig.), 195n1; Italian American, 18, 19, 39, 48–49, 73–74, 111–17, 193n7; portrayal of grace and salvation, 39, 163–66, 164 (fig.), 168, 170, 198nn1, 2

fine arts: American Catholics' interest in, 40–46, 50, 174; American Protestants' interest in, 41, 42–43; music, 3, 34–35, 41–42, 159–63. *See also* painting(s); sculpture(s)

Finnegans Wake (Joyce), 197n1

First Communion, 172 (fig.), 186

folk religion, 13–15, 16, 38, 79

Ford, John, 194n3; *The Fugitive*, 149, 151 (fig.)

forgiveness, 10, 115

Francesco de Maineri, Gian, *Christ Carrying the Cross*, 158 (fig.)

Franciscans, San Xavier Church reestablished by, 36–37

Francis of Assisi, St., 113, 152

Francis Xavier, St., 36

Frederick I (Frederick Barbarosa, Holy Roman Emperor), 27, 29

friend, versus king, image of God as, 43

Fugitive, The (film), 149, 151 (fig.)

fundamentalists, attitude toward sexuality of Jesus, 74, 116

gender: correlations with the Madonna Scale, 104. *See also* women

General Social Surveys (NORC), 40–42, 51–52, 106–7, 144, 168–69, 193n8

God, 5, 8–9, 17, 77, 123; images of, 43–44, 83, 85, 91, 176; love of (*see* love of God); Mother Love of (*see* Mother Love of God); people haunted by, 160; portrayed in the Bible as present on the wedding night, 70; presence of (*see* presence of God); stories of, 102; views on nature of, 169

Godfather films, 48–49

God Scale, 104

gothic churches, 33

Gounod, Charles-François, *Faust*, 19, 162–63, 168

government, Catholic attitude toward, 129–30

grace, 7, 75, 77–78, 102; and Catholic sensibility, 1, 10, 169–70, 174; and the liturgical imagination, 46; presence of, 13, 184, 187; relationship to feminism, 107; stories of in literature and film, 163–68, 198n1; stories of in music, 159–63

Grace Scale, 43–44, 107, 145

Great Britain: early nature religions of, 11–12; European Values Study, 130–32, 196n13; International Social Survey Program research, 127–28, 196n10, 197n7; Sarum rite marriage ritual, 61, 86

Great Depression, role in Farrell's *Studs Lonigan*, 118–19

Great St. Martin Church (Köln), 25, 33

Greene, Graham, 20, 184; *The Power and the Glory*, 19, 39, 147, 149, 152, 156, 168

Gregorian chant, 33, 50

Gregory the Great, St. (Gregory I, pope), message to Augustine of Canterbury, 11–12, 13, 15, 17, 36, 46

Hardy, Thomas, *Tess of the d'Urbervilles*, 166

Harrison, Paul, 141–42

Hassler, Jon, 20, 121, 156

Hauptbahnhof (railroad station), in Köln, 31

Heaney, Seamus, 140

Heart of Darkness (Conrad), 112

Heemskerck, Maerten van, 71, 86

hierarchical arrangement, of statues in San Xavier Church, 37–38

hierarchy, 179; as a characteristic of Catholicism, 137–38; and parish clergy, 147–48

high schools, Catholic, achievement test scores, 133–35

high tradition, Catholic, sociological model of, 76–86; applied to sexuality in marriage, 76, 78, 79–86

high tradition, in world religions, 76–77

holiness, desire for in *Mean Streets* character, 113, 115

Holy Family Parish church, Chicago, 177 (fig.)

Holy Orders, sacrament of, for women, 107–8, 155

Holy Spirit, 91, 184

homosexual marriages, Irish and Dutch attitudes toward compared, 132

hope, 161–62; stories of in music, 159–63

Hopkins, Gerard Manley, 184; "May Magnificat," 18, 92–94, 185–86

Household Saints (film), 39, 111 (fig.), 113, 193n7

Howatch, Susan, 66

humanism, Catholic, 71–72

humanity of Jesus: portrayal in Renaissance art, 70–74; present-day denial of, 194n4

human love, 7, 10; as metaphor for divine love, 7–8, 9–10, 56. See also erotic desire; sexual behavior/sexuality

human nature, as fundamentally good, 169; place of erotic desire, 55–56

human rights, violation of, 17–18

Hungary, International Social Survey Program research, 127–28, 196n10

iconoclasm, 72

idolatry, 5, 13–15

imagery, religious, 18; negative relationship to church attendance among Protestants, 44; positive relationship to church attendance among Catholics, 43–44; use in Scorsese's films, 113, 116–17

imagery, sexual, 55–56, 57, 63, 70–74. *See also* erotic desire
imagination: analogical, 50, 194n11 (*see also* imagination, Catholic); dialectical, 8, 50, 194n11; religious, 4 (*see also* imagination, Catholic; imagination, Protestant); relationship to feminism, 107; sacramental, 108
imagination, Catholic, 1–21, 31, 85, 183–87; compared to the Protestant imagination, 5, 8–9; image of Mary as distinctive in, 91–96, 101; Irish Catholic variety, Tracy on, 139; presence of God in all creation as key component (*see* presence of God); and the priest as sacrament, 147–48; reflected in Catholic approach to community, 125, 133, 138–47; reflected in the stories contained in churches, 34–39; relationship to interest in the fine arts, 43–46; of Scorsese, 117. *See also* sensibility, Catholic
imagination, Protestant, 20–21, 192n8; compared to the Catholic imagination, 5, 8–9
immanence of God, 5, 77
immigrants, 126, 138, 143–44
Incarnation, the: doctrine of, 4; and the sexuality of Jesus, 71
individualism, 124–25
industrial society, 123, 125
intellectuals, contemporary Catholic, 99–100
International Social Survey Program, 127–30, 132, 143–45
I Promissi Sposi (Manzoni), 149, 152–53

Ireland, 125, 197n6; Catholicism's use of nature religions, 10, 12, 15, 17; European Values Study, 130–32, 146, 196n13; International Social Survey Program research, 128, 132
Irish, the, 32, 47, 48–49, 146, 192n3
Irish Americans, 128; filmmakers, 194n3; literature of, 117–21; portrayal in Farrell's novels, 117–21
Ironweed (Kennedy), 121
Isaiah, Book of, 77
Islam, high and popular traditions, 77
Italian Americans, 118, 128; filmmakers, 18, 19, 48–49, 73–74, 111–17, 193n7; portrayal in films, 48–49, 111–16
Italian and Irish Filmmakers in America (Lourdeaux), 112, 113
Italy, 125; importance of festivals, 48–49; International Social Survey Program research, 128
It's a Wonderful Life (film), 112

Jagodzinski, Wolfgang, 191n1
Jerome, St., feast of, 14
Jesuitinkirche, in Mannheim, Germany, 33, 193n6
Jesuits, 17, 36, 193n6
Jesus: divinity of defined by the Arian and Monophysite heresies, 71; humanity of portrayed in Renaissance art, 70–74; humanity of denied in present day, 194n4; and sexuality, 56, 72–75, 116
Jesus Scale, 104
Jews, 77, 107, 144

John of the Cross (Juan de la Cruz),
St., 57, 59–61, 75, 86, 184
John Paul II (pope), 56, 100,
148–49; *Familiaris Consortio*,
79–80
John XXIII (pope), 26, 150 (fig.)
Joseph and the Wife of Potiphar
(Cignani), 66–67, 68 (fig.)
Joyce, James, 138–40, 197n1
Juan de la Cruz (John of the Cross),
St., 57, 59–61, 75, 86, 184
Judaism, 77, 107, 144
judge, versus lover, image of God
as, 43
Jutes, the, missionaries to, 11–12

Kane, Eileen, 193n5
Kazantzakis, Nikos, *The Last
Temptation of Christ*, 73–74, 116
Keitel, Harvey, 113, 114 (fig.)
Kennedy, William, *Ironweed*, 121
king, versus friend, image of God
as, 43
Kings, Book of, 77
Kirkegaard, Søren, 49, 194n11
Köln, 23–32, 36, 193n3; Cathe-
dral (Dom), 22 (fig.), 23–24, 25,
26–32, 33, 36, 38, 46, 170,
192n2; Shrine of the Magi, 25,
27–29, 28 (fig.), 31, 34; history,
24–26
"Kölner," versus "Kölnsch," 193n3

lapsed ("cultural") Catholics, 3
Last Catholic in America
(Powers), 121
Lastman, Pieter, *The Wedding
Night of Tobias and Sarah*, 67, 69
(fig.), 70
Last Temptation of Christ, The
(film), 73–74, 116–17

Last Temptation of Christ, The
(Kazantzakis), 73–74, 116
Lewis, Sinclair, 117
literature: Irish American, 117–21;
portrayal of erotic desire, 66;
portrayal of grace and salvation,
166–68, 170; portrayal of
priests, 147, 149, 152–54, 156,
168, 198nn8, 11. *See also Diary
of a Country Priest; Power and the
Glory, The*
Little Street, The (Vermeer), 121,
122 (fig.)
liturgical year, 34, 49, 50
liturgy: link with the fine arts,
44–46; as opposed to the liturgical imagination, 46; portrayal
in Farrell's novels, 120
Lodge, David, 20, 166–68; *Paradise News*, 166–68; *Therapy*,
49–50, 168
Lourdeaux, Lee, 112, 113, 117,
195n3
love of God (divine love), 2;
human love as metaphor for,
7–8, 9–10; lives of saints as stories of, 38–39; metaphors for,
75, 153; sexual imagery as
metaphor for, 55–56, 63
lover, versus judge, image of God
as, 43
Luther, Martin, 129

Madonna and child, images of, 4,
96; Bottega's *Madonna and Child*,
88 (fig.); Madonna of Milan in
Köln Cathedral, 29, 30 (fig.);
Our Lady of Guadalupe not
seen as, 14; portrayal of infant
Jesus, 70
Madonna Scale, 101, 103–6

Madonnas That Maim (Carroll), 20

Mamene, shrine of, 140

Manza, Jeff, analysis of voting patterns, 144–45

Manzoni, Alessandro, *I Promissi Sposi*, 149, 152–53

marriage: Catholic and Protestant attitudes compared, 131–32; as a sacrament, 7–8, 55, 73; Sarum rite, 61. *See also* sexual behavior/sexuality; spouse(s)

Martha and Mary: Jesus' relationship with, 73; in *Last Temptation of Christ*, 117

Martini, Cardinal Carlo Maria, 198n8

Martinkirche, in Bamberg, Germany, 193n6

Mary (mother of Jesus), 3–4, 129; abuse of and concern for, 99–100; artwork depicting (*see* Madonna and child; Pieta, the); Catholic imagination captured by stories of, 95–96, 98–102; image of among young people, 101, 103–6, 185; May crowning, 100, 186; as metaphor for the Mother Love of God, 16, 90–96, 105–6; present-day persistence of devotion to, 101–3; Our Lady of Guadalupe, 14

master, versus spouse, image of God as, 43

maternal dimension of God, 91. *See also* Mother Love of God

May crowning, 100, 186

"May Magnificat" (Hopkins), 18, 92–94, 185–86

McCready, William, 100

McGriel, Micheal, 140

Mean Streets (film), 18, 19, 49, 111, 113–16, 114 (fig.)

Meditations from a Moving Chair (Dubus), 2

mercy, need for in human love, 10

metaphor(s), 5–10, 13, 77, 90–91, 120, 192n5, 194n3; abuse of, 99–100; in Catholic churches, 34; Catholic religious imagination rooted in, 19–20; for God's love, 7–8, 9–10, 55–56, 63, 153; Mary as, 16, 90–96, 98–102, 105–6

Methodists, married to Catholics, Madonna Scale score, 106

Methodius, St., 17

Mexicans: importance of festivals to, 48; Our Lady of Guadalupe, 14

Michelangelo: Catholic puritans' treatment of figures, 62, 72, 195n5; *Pieta*, 96, 97 (fig.)

Middle Ages: Catholic clergy, 13, 80; Mary metaphor in, 95–96

minority students, in Catholic high schools, 134

miracle plays, 34

mission church, San Xavier Church as, 36–38

modernity, 2; Italian family system not affected by, 128; revolt against seen in papal encyclicals' approach to community, 124–25

Modern Language Association, 119

monastery, Irish, established in Köln, 25

Monophysite heresy, 71

Moon Gaffney (Sylvester), 121

morality plays, 34

mother, versus father, image of God as, 43

motherhood, experience of, 102;
and the Madonna Scale, 103–4
Mother Love of God, Mary as a
metaphor for, 16, 90–96,
105–6; abuse of and concern
for, 99–100; present-day persistence of, 101–3
mother symbols, universality of in
religion, 101
Mozart, Wolfgang Amadeus,
162–63, 184; Piano Concerto
no. 26, 159–61, 162, 168
music, 3, 34–35, 41–42, 159–63;
oratorios and opera, 3, 34–35,
161–63
myths, structure of, 191n3

Napoleonic wars, effect on Köln, 25
narrative. *See* stories
National Catholic Register, attack
on *Breaking the Waves*, 198n1
National Opinion Research Center (NORC). *See* General Social
Surveys
Native American customs,
combined with Catholic customs, 38
Nativity scene, 102
nature religions, 10–15, 91
neighborhoods, 143–44; importance in Italian American films,
112–13, 115, 117, 121; parishes
as in the United States, 125–27,
196n9; as settings for Irish
American authors, 118–21
neo-Platonism, on sexual desire,
61–62
Netherlands, the, International
Social Survey Program research,
127–28, 132, 196n10

networks, social: Catholic and
Protestant views of, 125–32. *See
also* community
Nicholas of Verdun, 29, 184
NORC (National Opinion Re-
search Center). *See* General So-
cial Surveys
Normans, the, 94–95
North of Hope (Hassler), 121
Nothing Sacred (TV show), 156
Notre Dame de Chartres, 18
Notre Dame de Paris, 33, 95

O'Brien, Pat, 154, 156, 198n9
Ocean City, Md., sand rendition of
the Pieta, 182 (fig.)
O'Connor, Edwin, 20, 153, 156;
Edge of Sadness, 121, 147, 168
oligarchy, Acton's "iron law of,"
197n3
O'Malley, John W., 70–71, 72,
74
"One Dark Night Fired with
Love's Urgent Longings" (John
of the Cross), 57, 59–61
O'Neill, Thomas ("Tip"), 142,
156
opera, 3, 41–42, 161–63
oratorios, 34
ordination of women, support for,
107–8, 155
Orsi, Robert, 48–49
Orwell, George, 141
O'Siadhail, Micheal, 47
Otto IV (Holy Roman Em-
peror), 27
"Our Lady," cathedrals dedicated
to, 94–95. *See also* Mary (mother
of Jesus)
Our Lady of Guadalupe, 14

Our Lord of the Happy Death
(Bomfim), festival of, in Brazil,
14–15
Ozment, Stephen, 13

pagan religions, 10–15, 17, 95
painting(s), 3, 70–74; Bottega's
Madonna and Child, 88 (fig.);
Cignani's *Joseph and the Wife of
Potiphar*, 66–67, 69 (fig.);
Rubens's *Bathsheba at the Fountain*, 58 (fig.)
papacy, 137–38, 179, 186–87; encyclicals' emphasis on community, 123–25, 127; portrayal in
West's novels, 149. *See also individual popes by name*
Paradise News (Lodge), 166–68
parents, as socializing influence,
175–76
parish, the: de facto subsidiarity,
143; as neighborhood community,
125–27, 196n9; as setting for
Irish American authors, 118–21
Parsifal (Wolfram von Eschenbach), 81
patronage, expressions of in St.
Peter's, 35
peasant community, 123; in urban
context, neighborhood parish
seen as, 125–27
Peter Grimes (Britten), 163
Piano Concerto no. 26 (Mozart),
159–61, 162, 168
Pieta, the, 35, 96; of Michelangelo,
96, 97 (fig.); sand rendition of,
182 (fig.)
pilgrimage(s), depicted in Lodge's
Therapy, 49–50
pilgrims, to Köln, 31

Pius XI (pope), 197n5
place, sense of in the Catholic
imagination, 139–41. *See also* sacred place[s]/space[s]
Platonism, 192n7
poetic Catholicism, 76. *See also*
popular tradition, Catholic
Poland, International Social Survey Program, 196n11
politics, Catholic attitudes toward:
compared to Protestant attitudes, 130–31; perceived and
actual, 144–46
polyphonic masses, 34
Pontifical Commission on the
Family, 75
popular tradition, Catholic, sociological model of, 76–86; applied
to sexuality in marriage, 76, 78,
79–86
popular tradition, in world religions, 76–77
pornographic, the, borderland between the erotic and, 62, 65
power: Acton on, 197n3; in communal religious structure,
Protestant and Catholic views
of, 141–42, 197n4
Power and the Glory, The (Greene),
19, 39, 147, 149, 152, 156, 168
Powers, J. F., 20, 121, 153, 156
Powers, John R.: *Last Catholic in
America*, 121; "Patent Leather
Shoes," 100
prayer, frequency of, correlation
with the Madonna Scale, 101,
103–4
presence of God, 2; illustrated
by Köln and its Dom, 24;
stories of in churches, 34–39;

presence of God (*continued*)
symbolized by the pope, 187; in
the world, 5, 16–17, 77–78
Priest (film), 147, 154, 198n10
priests. *See* clergy, Catholic
procreation (conception of children), sexual pleasure for purpose of: in Augustinian and neo-
Platonic tradition, 60, 61–62; as
Catholic teaching, 75
prosaic Catholicism, 76. *See also*
high tradition, Catholic
Protestantism/Protestant, 5, 7–8,
43–44, 52, 107, 192n8, 193n8;
approach to salvation seen in literature, film, and opera, 163,
164–65, 166, 198n2; on Catholic image of Mary, 91, 106;
ethic, compared with the Catholic ethic, 131–32; high and
popular traditions, 77; imagination, 5, 8–9, 20–21, 192n8; interest in fine arts, 42, 44; laity's
relationship to the clergy, 155;
Reformation, 8–9, 13, 123;
treatment of sexual imagery in
Renaissance art, 72; view of
communal religious power,
141–42, 197n4; views on human
relationships and social issues,
compared with Catholic views,
51, 127–33, 144–45; worldview
compared with Catholic, 169
proto-love, 55–56
Proudhon, Pierre-Joseph, 196n8
Puerto Rico, First Communion,
172 (fig.)
puritanism, 62, 65, 72

Rahner, Karl, 167
railroad, in Köln, 29, 31

Raphael: Madonnas painted by,
96; *Virgin and Child* attributed
to, ii (fig.)
reality: Catholic sensibility responsible for view of, 170, 174, 186;
seen as a sacrament, 1–2
Real Presence, doctrine of, 4, 185
Reformation, the, 8–9, 13, 123
Reinald von Dassel (archbishop of
Köln), 27, 29
relics, in Köln Cathedral's Shrine
of the Magi, 27, 29
Religion as Poetry (Greeley), 3, 43
Renaissance art, 70–74, 96. *See
also individual artists and works*
Ricoeur, Paul, 79
rituals: developed by parishioners
of San Xavier Church, 38; role
in Italian American films, 113
Roman Empire, Köln's role in,
24–25
Romanesque church architecture,
23, 24–25, 33
Roncalliplatz, in Köln, 26
Rubens, Peter Paul, *Bathsheba at
the Fountain*, 58 (fig.)

sacrament(s)/sacramentality, 1–2,
7–8, 55, 79, 102, 116, 137; First
Communion, 172 (fig.); marriage as a, 55, 73; presence of
God in, 185; the priest as,
147–48, 154–57
sacred place(s)/space(s), 17, 21,
33–34, 36, 38; Catholic
churches as, 27, 46–47
sacred time, 34, 36, 38, 49
sadness: in Mozart's Piano Concerto no. 26, 159–61; portrayed in Verdi's *La Traviata*,
161–62

saints: celebrated by parishioners of San Xavier Church, 38; lives as stories of God's love, 38–39

salvation, 159–70; stories of in literature and film, 163–68, 170; stories of in music, 159–63. *See also* grace

Samuel, Book of, 77

Santiago de Compestela, Spain, 26, 194n11; festival of depicted in Lodge's *Therapy*, 49–50

Santo Domingo de Silos, monks of, 50

San Xavier (St. Xavier del Bac; White Dove in the Desert) Mission, in Arizona, 36–38, 185, 188 (fig.)

Sarum rite, marriage ritual, 61, 86

Savoca, Nancy, *Household Saints*, 39, 110 (fig.), 113, 193n7

Saxons, the, missionaries to, 11–12

Schlossman, Berry, 197n1

schools. *See* education

Schuck, Michael, 123–24, 144

science, relationship to religion, 2–3

Scorsese, Martin, 113, 116, 118, 126, 184; *The Last Temptation of Christ*, 73–74, 116–17; *Mean Streets*, 18, 19, 49, 111, 113–16

Scripture(s): Baptist insistence on literal inerrancy of, 197n4; Book of Tobit, 70; human passion as metaphor for divine passion, 61; New Testament scenes depicting Mary seized upon by the Catholic imagination, 95–96; prosaic and poetic traditions, 77; Song of Songs, 7, 57, 61, 77

sculpture(s): Michelangelo's *Pieta*, 96, 97 (fig.); of St. Theresa in divine ecstasy, by Bernini, 54 (fig.), 57, 63, 64 (fig.), 65

Second Vatican Council, 3, 100, 154, 185

self, communitarian understanding of, 124–25

sensibility, Catholic, 1, 6, 10, 75, 183–87; on communal religious structure, compared with Protestant sensibility, 141–42; and devotion to Our Lady of Guadalupe, 14; found in literature and films about salvation, 163–68; found in music, 161–63; image of Mary as distinctive in, 91; origins, 173–80. *See also* imagination, Catholic

sexual abuse of children, 148

sexual behavior/sexuality, 17, 75–85, 129, 174, 186; Augustine on, 60, 61–62, 75–76, 80–81, 85–86; innuendos in Brazilian feast of Bomfim, 15; in marriage, 75–76, 78, 79–86, 101, 103, 104–5; passion as metaphor for divine passion, 8, 9, 57, 59–61; for purpose of procreation, 60, 61–62, 75; satisfaction, role in religious sensibility, 176, 178, 184; in Scorsese's films, 116–17; traditional Catholic attitudes toward, 60, 61–62

sexual imagery. *See* imagery, sexual; erotic desire

sexuality of Jesus, 72–75

Shakespeare, William, 152

Shea, John, 77

shrimping fleet, blessing of, 136 (fig.)

Shrine of the Magi, in the Köln Dom, 25, 27–29, 28 (fig.), 31, 34

shrines, pagan, in England, Gregory I's advice on, 11–12

Slavic culture, efforts of Cyril and Methodius to adjust to, 17

social ethic, Catholic, 123–24

social issues, Catholics' views on, 174, 184–85; compared with Protestant and Jewish views, 127–32, 144–45

Socialist Realism, 119

socialization agents, of Catholic sensibility, 173–80

sociology, 18, 20, 132; views on Catholic communalism, 123–25, 127, 132–33

Song of Songs, 7, 57, 61, 77

Southern Baptist Convention, 197n4

space, Joyce's stories organized around specific pattern of, 139–40, 197n1. *See also* sacred place(s)/space(s)

Spain, International Social Survey Program, 196n11

spirituality: in the Irish Catholic imagination, 139; liturgical, 45–46

spiritual poverty, in Farrell's *Studs Lonigan*, 118–19

spouse(s): versus master, image of God as, 43, 85; non-Catholic, strength of Mary image among, 106; positive experiences with, correlation with the Madonna Scale, 103, 104–5; as primary religious socializers, 176, 179. *See also* marriage

St. Peter's Basilica, in Vatican City, 26, 33, 35

St. Peter's Cathedral, in London, 26

St. Xavier del Bac (San Xavier; White Dove in the Desert) Mission, Az., 36–38, 185, 188 (fig.)

Steinberg, Leo, 70-71, 72, 74

stereotypes, of Italian Americans in films, 111-12

stories, 4–5, 44; churches as treasure houses of, 34–39, 46–47; of God's relationship with the world and with humankind, 133; of Mary, 92, 95–96, 98–99; religious sensibility transmitted through telling of, 175, 180, 187; sacred time and sacred space bound together in, 36, 38; told in the Third World, 191n3

structure, as a characteristic of Catholicism, 137–38. *See also* hierarchy

Studs Lonigan (Farrell), 118–19, 120

Study of Young Catholics, 175–76, 178

subsidiarity, principle of, 142–43, 197n5

Suger of Saint-Denis, 193n5

suicide, Catholic and Protestant attitudes compared, 131

Sullivan, Terry, 101

superstition(s), 5, 8, 13, 16, 79, 99, 191n1

Suttles, Gerald, 126–27

Sylvester, Harry, *Moon Gaffney*, 121

tenderness: evolutionary development of, 56; of God, reflected in Mary, 91, 101

Tenebrae services, *Finnegans Wake* seen as structured around, 197n1

Tess of the d'Urbervilles (Hardy), 166

theologians, weak influence on Catholic sensibility, 179–80

Therapy (Lodge), 49–50, 168
Theresa, St., divine ecstasy of, 57; Bernini sculpture, 54 (fig.), 57, 63, 64 (fig.), 65
Thomas Aquinas, St., 25, 129
Thornbirds (McCullough), 147
Tillich, Paul, 8–9
time, sacred, 34, 36, 38, 49
Tobit, Book of, 70
Tono Odham Native Americans, 37
Tracy, David, 5–7, 8, 20, 43, 139
tradition, Catholic, sociological models of, 76–86; applied to sexuality in marriage, 76, 78, 79–86
transcendence of God, accentuated by Protestant theologians, 5
Traviata, La (Verdi), 19, 161–62, 168
Trollope, Anthony, 66
Turner, Marvin, 5

Ulysses (Joyce), 139–40
Under the Son of Satan (Bernanos), 39, 156; film version, 198n12
United States: European Values Study, 130–32, 196n13; International Social Survey Program research, 127–28, 196n10
Updike, John, 66

Van Heemskerck, Maerten, 71, 86
Vatican II (Second Vatican Council), 3, 100, 154, 185
Verba, Sidney, 95
Verdi, Giuseppe, *La Traviata*, 19, 161–62, 168
Vermeer, Jan, 121, 184; *The Little Street*, 121, 122 (fig.)
Villon, François, hymn to Mary, 98–99
Virgin and Child (attrib. Raphael), ii (fig.)

von Trier, Lars, *Breaking the Waves*, 39, 163–66, 164 (fig.), 168, 198nn1, 2

Warner, Marina, 105
Watson, Emily, 163, 164 (fig.)
Weber, Max, 123, 124, 125, 196n7
Wedding Night of Tobias and Sarah, The (Lastman), 67, 69 (fig.), 70
West, Morris, 149
White Dove in the Desert (San Xavier; St. Xavier del Bac) Mission, Az., 36–38, 185, 188 (fig.)
Whitehead, Alfred North, 4
witchcraft, 13
Wolfram von Eschenbach, 61, 81
women, 91, 105, 176, 178; confidant relationships with priests, 155–57, 178; equal rights and opportunities for, 106–7, 174, 176; mixed views of Church leadership, 107–8; priestly ordination of, support for, 107–8, 155
World Values Study. *See* European Values Study
worldview, Catholic, 174, 184; in papal encyclicals' approach to community, 124–25, 196n8; strength of Catholic, 132–33
worldview, General Social Survey questions on, 168–69
World War II, effect on Köln, 23–24, 25–26

young adults: conversations with priests and return to the Church, 155; Mary image among, 101, 103–6; studies of, 128–29, 175–76, 178
Young Studs, The (Farrell), 120

Compositor: Impressions Book and Journal Services, Inc.
Text: Janson 10/15
Display: Janson